"Ben Lowe tells you how to keep your passion for justice alive while avoiding burnout and compassion fatigue. He has learned the hard way how to balance the journey inward and the journey outward. Ben is wise beyond his years. May God send us more activists like him."
David Neff, former editor in chief of *Christianity Today*

"Ben Lowe is a leader for our times. He combines his love for Jesus, people and justice in a way that offers hope. This book challenges us to persevere as faithful activists."
Leroy Barber, global executive director, Word Made Flesh, and author of *Everyday Missions*

"Drawing on his experience as a student activist, environmentalist, congressional candidate and multicultural neighbor, Ben Lowe provides helpful guidance on how concerned Christians can live as salt and light in a troubled world. More importantly, he offers hard-won wisdom on how to sustain and rebuild spiritual integrity that can nurture youthful enthusiasm into mature faithfulness and effective service. *Doing Good Without Giving Up* will be appreciated by new believers and long-time Christ-followers alike."
Galen Carey, vice president, National Association of Evangelicals

"As followers of Jesus, we are called to seek social justice and the common good—in short, to change the world. Few young leaders have done as much or worked as hard toward this goal as Ben Lowe has. In his inspirational and thought-provoking book *Doing Good Without Giving Up*, Ben shows us how to faithfully pursue social justice without losing heart when the change we seek doesn't happen as quickly or as easily as we might hope. Anyone who seeks to change the world for the better should read this book. A new generation of faith leaders like Ben Lowe give me real hope."
Jim Wallis, president, Sojourners

"Activists and revolutionaries don't always end well. Some burn out, some sell out, some buy in. Others destroy their families, forget their God or become obsessed with themselves. Ben Lowe mixes the idealistic passion of youth with the field-tested wisdom of an elder. He'll help you rekindle your fire, reclaim your innocence and fall in love with Jesus all over again. This book guides you both in how to start and how to end well as you join with God in the revolutionary, tiring, holy work of building a better world."
Shane Claiborne, author and activist

DOING
GOOD
WITHOUT
GIVING
UP

SUSTAINING SOCIAL ACTION IN
A WORLD THAT'S HARD TO CHANGE

BEN LOWE

Foreword by AJITH FERNANDO

IVP Books

An imprint of InterVarsity Press
Downers Grove, Illinois

InterVarsity Press
P.O. Box 1400, Downers Grove, IL 60515-1426
www.ivpress.com
email@ivpress.com

InterVarsity Press® is the book-publishing division of InterVarsity Christian Fellowship/USA®, a movement of students and faculty active on campus at hundreds of universities, colleges and schools of nursing in the United States of America, and a member movement of the International Fellowship of Evangelical Students. For information about local and regional activities, write Public Relations Dept., InterVarsity Christian Fellowship/USA, 6400 Schroeder Rd., P.O. Box 7895, Madison, WI 53707-7895, or visit the IVCF website at www.intervarsity.org.

All Scripture quotations, unless otherwise indicated, are taken from THE HOLY BIBLE, NEW INTERNATIONAL VERSION®, NIV® Copyright © 1973, 1978, 1984, 2011 by Biblica, Inc.™ Used by permission. All rights reserved worldwide.

While all stories in this book are true, some names and identifying information in this book have been changed to protect the privacy of the individuals involved.

"Prophets of a Future Not Our Own" by Ken Untener is reprinted with permission from Little Books of the Diocese of Saginaw.

Cover design: Cindy Kiple
Interior design: Beth McGill
Images: © 4x6/iStockphoto

ISBN 978-0-8308-3679-6 (print)
ISBN 978-0-8308-9672-1 (digital)

Printed in the United States of America ∞

Library of Congress Cataloging-in-Publication Data
Lowe, Ben, 1984-
  Doing good without giving up : sustaining social action in a world that's hard to change / Ben Lowe.
    pages cm
  Includes bibliographical references.
  ISBN 978-0-8308-3679-6 (pbk. : alk. paper)
1. Christian life. 2. Social action. 3. Christian ethics. 4. Service (Theology) 5. Church and social problems. 6. Social service—Religious aspects—Christianity. I. Title.
  BV4520.L585 2014
  261.8'32--dc23
                                                                                    2014022811

P 23 22 21 20 19 18 17 16 15 14 13 12 11 10 9 8 7 6 5 4 3 2 1
Y 33 32 31 30 29 28 27 26 25 24 23 22 21 20 19 18 17 16 15 14

To God,

with thanksgiving

for your unfailing presence

in our lives

and in this world.

Emmanuel—

now and forever.

CONTENTS

FOREWORD

IN MY YOUTH, I BELONGED to the evangelical minority in a mainline church in Sri Lanka and was dismayed by the lack of emphasis on evangelism in the church. With my commitment to Christ in my mid-teens also came a burden to reach the lost with the gospel. I viewed with suspicion the strong emphasis on social action and justice that characterized the understanding of mission among many in my church, almost to the exclusion of emphasis on the need to take the gospel to lost people. In fact, the idea that people without Christ were lost was viewed with disdain by many leaders in our church.[1] I had inherited the attitudes of mutual suspicion that existed during the era of the battle for mission that characterized liberal-evangelical relations in the last century.

Yet from my teen years I was burdened with a love for the poor and with a sense of a call to serve them. This never left me; and during the past three and a half decades my ministry has been primarily with the urban poor. As a youth I developed a growing unease and anger over the class distinctions and inequality that existed in our society. I knew Christians must address these issues. When I was in my mid-twenties I was exposed to the writings of evangelicals, like John Stott and Ron Sider, which showed me biblical Christians can hold a commitment to evangelism alongside a commitment to social justice.

God called me to work in an evangelistic organization, Youth for Christ.

This meant that the primary agenda of our movement was evangelism. But as we began working with the poor we realized that our lifestyle and ministry must take into account the glaring inequalities and injustices that exist in society. According to the laws of our land, those doing evangelism cannot be involved in major social projects because of the perceived possibility of alluring people to Christianity using material incentives. But when one works with the poor one cannot ignore the huge social needs they face. As we were committed to the nurture of those who came to Christ in our ministry, we soon found that doing something about their needs was an important part of that nurture. So education and vocational guidance, guidance on how people could avail themselves of opportunities available through government and other groups, and many other such social emphases became part of our program.

Nurturing new believers is an important part of the program of an evangelistic ministry. As the biblical lifestyle includes commitment to social responsibility, this became a part of our nurturing curriculum. Some who had been nurtured in our work opted for careers in social action–related causes. It has been our joy to see many youth emerging from our ministry becoming active in macrosocial projects, which evangelistic organizations cannot be engaged in. It has also been my joy to act as an encourager to a few biblical Christians in Sri Lanka and elsewhere who have sensed a primary call to the fields of social and political action. As for me, my primary work remains in the field of evangelism and nurturing those responding to and involved in it.

Yet in the evangelical community there still remains a suspicion that comes from the old "evangelism versus social concern" wars. Those of us who are involved in evangelism are still accused of being insensitive to human need, and biblical Christians involved in social concern are accused of being unbiblical. For many years I have been wishing for the emergence of a crop of younger Christians belonging to the "postwar" generation who focus on obeying what the Bible says and the call God gives them without letting the prejudices of a past era cloud their thinking.

Ben Lowe represents this generation. I have known him from the time he was a little boy and watched him grow into a sensitive Christian serious about doing God's will. In this book he demonstrates an unflinching commitment to the urgent need to share the gospel with all people so they may receive eternal salvation (that relates to my primary vocation). And he writes out of his deep biblical conviction that the church must be involved in social action (that relates to his primary vocation). How much the church needs the deep biblical reflection along with thoroughgoing and sometimes unpleasant application that we see in this book! In reading this book it was my delight to sit at the feet of this young teacher and learn from him.

Perhaps one of the greatest values of this book is that it is a very practical book loaded with examples of positive and negative experiences from Ben's own life. It practically applies key biblical values to the work of social involvement and shows how these are important aspects of Christian discipleship. Among such values are the primacy of love; the need to be prophetic in addressing the needs of the world, to respond to opposition Christianly, to avoid all forms of idolatry and to repent when we go wrong; and the importance of sabbath rest, of contemplation and of community life.

Will this emphasis on social concern result in the neglect of evangelism by the church? After all, there are so many social needs in the world that even if the whole church gives itself devotedly to this work there would still be so much more to do. Where's the time or energy for evangelism? If we realize that people are lost without Christ, that would not happen. We would do all we can, amidst our busy schedules of meeting human need, to ensure that all people everywhere have an opportunity to meet their greatest human need, their greatest right: their need and right to know the salvation their Creator has won for them.

Ajith Fernando
Teaching Director, Youth for Christ, Sri Lanka

BEGIN HERE

Prophets of a Future Not Our Own

It helps, now and then, to step back and take a long view.

The kingdom of God is not only beyond our efforts, it is even beyond our vision.

We accomplish in our lifetime only a tiny fraction of the magnificent enterprise that is God's work. Nothing we do is complete, which is a way of saying that the kingdom always lies beyond us.

No statement says all that could be said.

No prayer fully expresses our faith.

No confession brings perfection.

No pastoral visit brings wholeness.

No program accomplishes the Church's mission.

No set of goals and objectives includes everything.

This is what we are about:

We plant the seeds that one day will grow.

We water seeds already planted, knowing that they hold future promise.

We lay foundations that will need further development.

We provide yeast that produces effects far beyond our capabilities.

We cannot do everything, and there is a sense of liberation in realizing that.

This enables us to do something, and to do it very well.

It may be incomplete, but it is a beginning, a step along the way, an opportunity for the Lord's grace to enter and do the rest.

We may never see the end results, but that is the difference between the master builder and the worker.

We are workers, not master builders; ministers not messiahs.

We are prophets of a future not our own.[1]

PART ONE

RENEWING OUR MISSION

1

WAIT, DON'T GIVE UP!

Let us not become weary in doing good,
for at the proper time we will reap
a harvest if we do not give up.

GALATIANS 6:9

THIS IS A BOOK FOR PEOPLE who are struggling to change the world.

I'm one of those people. If you're reading this, then you're probably one too.

We aspire to make a positive difference in the world around us—in our communities, on our campuses, in our churches, in the nation and beyond—and that's a good thing. We need more justice. We need more peace. We need more change.

As Christ-followers, we get to be part of God's redemptive work on earth. We get to be salt and light to a dark and decaying world. And we get to join God in his great mission of healing and transforming people, societies and all of creation.

It's an all-inclusive and all-encompassing mission, not just for full-time activists but for all of us: students, teachers, social workers, entrepreneurs, pastors, public servants, artists, scientists, office workers, health professionals, technicians, stay-at-home parents, retirees and everyone—including you.

This is good work. This is holy work. But it certainly isn't easy work. Change is hard no matter what field you're in.

As I travel across America working on issues of justice and compassion, I'm finding a lot of discouragement and disillusionment, and I'm witnessing many well-intentioned and once-passionate Christ-followers lose steam and become distracted, disengaged or in despair. How can we avoid becoming such casualties? How can we survive and even thrive as we pursue God's vision and mission in the world?

ALEX'S STORY

One of my role models in college was a student leader named Alex. Alex and I went to different Chicago-area universities, but I met him when he visited my campus to gather signatures for a petition to Congress on human trafficking. I hadn't heard much about the horrors of modern-day slavery yet (I thought that slavery no longer existed), but once he filled me in I eagerly signed the petition.

Alex was a passionate and visionary activist who many of us looked up to as a modern-day abolitionist. Before I knew him, Alex had spent a summer interning in Africa for an organization that worked with former child soldiers. He returned home from that experience fired up and eager to mobilize our generation to make a difference. Though still a full-time student, Alex threw himself into the cause: giving informational talks anywhere he could find an audience, traveling to participate in rallies, organizing groups to attend trainings, delivering petitions to elected officials in Washington, DC, and more. His efforts were inspiring and played a big role in my decision to get involved in student activism as well.

I lost touch with Alex for a while after he graduated, but I vaguely remembered hearing that he had gone on to work for an investment firm in downtown Chicago. We happened to cross paths recently, and I was eager to catch up. But Alex seemed almost sheepish to see me.

Visibly embarrassed, he confessed that he wasn't involved in social justice efforts anymore and mumbled something about having "sold out" to the system.

We didn't get to talk for very long before he had to go, but that unexpected encounter continues to trouble me. My main disappointment is not with Alex's job per se—working in the financial sector can be a calling from God and can be done faithfully and even prophetically—but that Alex himself felt that he had traded a lifestyle of pursuing justice for one of comfort and disengagement. I don't know how this came about. Perhaps he had college loans to pay back, or maybe he simply needed a break from activism. Whatever the reason, I hope Alex will get more involved again one day.

CHANGE IS HARD

Meaningful change—especially at the systemic or structural level of social action—can be hard and slow. We're facing big problems that require complex, comprehensive and often controversial solutions: poverty, hunger, climate change, immigration, education, abortion, pollution, health care, disease, human rights, slavery, nuclear proliferation, biodiversity loss, ethnic and religious persecution, and the list goes on.

Faithfully addressing these interconnected social and environmental crises requires all of us working together on multiple fronts.

As individuals we're called to continue reforming our lifestyles and consumption patterns to be just and compassionate. And as churches we're called to continue providing charity and reaching out to those who are struggling and marginalized. But we don't stop there. We may not think of ourselves as "activists," but all of us are called—in one way or another and in one place or another—to participate in social action, which includes both charity and justice. We're called to engage the public square and seek the common good. Values need to be cultivated, programs developed, policies implemented, laws passed, systems reformed and corruption eradicated.

The problem is that none of this happens overnight. And none of it happens without a struggle. So, what does faithful social action look like today, and how can we persevere in it over the long haul?

It's exciting to join a new cause or be part of a new movement. But the honeymoon phase eventually wears off, our idealism clashes with entrenched reality, and the consequences can be messy. Discouragement and disillusionment can be real enemies. Some of us continue to press onward, while others give up or give in to complacency.

Bethany Hoang of International Justice Mission makes a similar observation based on her work mobilizing Christians for social action:

> While many followers of Jesus are rising up with passion against injustice, this passion risks amounting to nothing more than a fad, a firecracker that explodes with great fanfare but quickly fades out. Even if we may initially explode with conviction, the excitement quickly dies and cannot sustain meaningful action. Instead of a lifelong obedience, the attempt to look injustice in the face and the magnitude of human need can easily bring nothing more than utter paralysis and even worse, despair.[1]

In our consumerist and media-saturated age there are also many mind- and heart-numbing distractions that can disconnect us from reality and draw us away from seeking first the kingdom of God (Matthew 6:24, 33). Distractions as embarrassingly shallow as video games, television, fashion, celebrities, sports, stock investments, weight and personal appearance can all too quickly metastasize into unhealthy obsessions. Even good and appropriate responsibilities, such as being a diligent student or providing for a family, can turn into idols. We live in a self-centered, narcissistic culture, and few escape unscathed.

Beyond the Honeymoon Phase

I can relate to these struggles.

As a Christian from the millennial generation, I'm striving to follow Jesus Christ in every area of life, from the private to the public and from the personal to the professional. Over the last decade this journey has led me to become increasingly involved in activism and advocacy, from working as a campus organizer and writing books to cofounding a nonprofit and running for US Congress. As I write, I'm living among refugees and immigrants, campaigning for affordable housing, and helping to spearhead a national advocacy initiative called Young Evangelicals for Climate Action.

Without a doubt this has been a good and God-filled journey. But, as I'll share throughout this book, it has also been a hard and wearying ride. Many of those who know me think that I'm full of passion and idealism—and by God's grace I usually am—but I've also struggled deeply and repeatedly with discouragement, exhaustion, anxiety and depression. There were days when I just didn't want to get out of bed, and there are still days when I don't want to. I often struggle with feeling overwhelmed at the magnitude and complexity of the problems, and I have to continually be on my guard against cynicism and bitterness.

So, I get it. Pursuing justice is hard, and the status quo can be slow to change. But this isn't a reason to give up or avoid getting involved. Rather, it's a challenge for us to persevere, for "suffering produces perseverance; perseverance, character; and character, hope. And hope does not put us to shame, because God's love has been poured out into our hearts through the Holy Spirit, who has been given to us" (Romans 5:3-5).

The world is full of darkness and decay. This is a harsh and wearisome reality, but the sooner we face up to it the better, for it's the very reason God sends us out as his witnesses. As John Stott once said: "We should not ask, 'What is wrong with the world?' for that diagnosis has already been given. Rather, we should ask, 'What has happened to the salt and light?'"[2]

Given all of this, how can we persevere in seeking justice over the long haul? The answers to this question, and the future of our social engagement, are largely shaped by whether we get the following two things right.

Fixing Our Expectations

First, we need to get our expectations right. We live in an instant and entitled society, and we're used to fast and dramatic results—fast food, overnight mailing, short lines, immediate answers on everything (thanks, Google), mind-blowing high-definition movies and high-speed Internet on all of our high-speed gadgets. It's hard to keep our attention. If something takes time or gets old, we quickly lose interest or upgrade to the next new thing.

This impatient and demanding mentality overflows into our social action as well. We want changing the world to be like an action-hero movie: exciting, satisfying and quickly resolved. The problem is that social change remains hard, slow and unpredictable. It's always been that way—just read the biblical prophets.

Seeking justice is a lot like fishing.

I live just outside Chicago, but I love visiting my grandmother in South Florida. Serious salt-water fishing there is hard work and takes considerable planning and preparation. I often spend the whole afternoon netting bait and rigging my gear so that I'm ready to go fishing the next morning.

And the catching is unpredictable. Some days on the water are slow, while others are so fast that I can barely keep up. I can be fishing in all the right places with all the right lures and bait, and still not know if something is going to bite. The right timing factors as much into fishing as it does into social change.

Although everyone wants to catch big fish, the real trophies are hard to come by. And when you finally hook into something big, there's a reasonable chance it will break the line or shake the hook and get away, which can be very disappointing. Sound enough like working on justice issues yet?

I often take friends fishing in Florida. Though I always caution against high expectations, they've all seen the photos of past big catches on my Facebook wall so they start out with great excitement and anticipation. After a couple slow hours on the water, however, many of them inevitably find it boring.

Part of the problem here is that *change* is being marketed very carelessly these days. I recently heard a Christian music concert advertised on the radio as "a night that could change the world forever." Really? This may be a catchy promotional tactic, but it's simply not true, and such irresponsible talk only further feeds into unhealthy expectations.

Seeking justice is not a fad or a hobby; it's an integral part of our Christian discipleship; it's a lifestyle and a lifelong pursuit. My millennial generation is particularly bad at this. One of our great weaknesses is that while we can be incredibly passionate, we lack staying power.

It's often and rightly said that few worthwhile endeavors are easy. We need to expect pursuing justice to be hard, slow and unpredictable. And then we need to stick with it anyway.

FIXING OUR PRIORITIES

Second, we have to order our priorities well or else we'll end up seeking justice in the wrong ways. As C. S. Lewis put it, "you can't get second things by putting them first. You get second things only by putting first things first."[3]

We want change in the world. And we desperately need it. But getting results is ultimately not the first priority in our social action— being faithful is. All Christians are called to action. But we define the success of our action by faithfulness, not effectiveness. In other words, achieving change is the "second thing" while attaining to faithfulness is the "first thing." We don't get change, at least not good and lasting change, by making it our priority; we get change by making faithfulness our priority.

"I am the vine; you are the branches," Jesus taught. "If you remain in me and I in you, you will bear much fruit; apart from me you can do nothing" (John 15:5). We're called to remain in Christ—to be faithful to him—and only by doing so will we be fruitful. Faithfulness leads to fruitfulness.

To be sure, this isn't an excuse for not expecting results. After all, Jesus teaches that by being faithful we *will* bear much fruit, even if we don't always get to see it or even if the results we do see don't always look like what we expected. Rather, it's a call to strive only for God-honoring results and only in God-honoring ways. Christians affirm that God is sovereign and in control of all things, and we trust his timing, his provision and his power. Our faith releases us from the compulsive drive to succeed in the eyes of the world and the corrupting fear of failing, and empowers us to do the right thing no matter what the cost or outcome. Seeking justice is about embracing the freedom of faithfulness rather than the necessity of success.

Pursuing effectiveness as our priority points people to ourselves and idolizes the change *we* seek. Pursuing faithfulness as our priority points people to Christ, who is the center of all we are and do, and is ultimately the best—if not only—way to bring about the change *God* seeks. Ultimately, justice is not about us; it's about God—his will, his ways and his timing.

WHY THIS BOOK

The heart of doing good and seeking justice is that we are called to define success by faithfulness and to press on in this calling even when things become hard or frustrating. This is the premise of the whole book. It may seem like a simple message to grasp, but it's a challenge to live out and sustain.

The rest of the book, then, is about exploring what this can look like in concrete and accessible ways. What does faithful social action look like today, and how can we persevere in it over the long haul?

I address this question in two parts. Part one, "Renewing Our Mission," focuses on how we can recalibrate our calling to social action, while part two, "Sustaining Our Action," explores key principles and practices for persevering in faithful praxis. A fundamental theme throughout both sections is that Jesus must remain at the center of all we are and do. At the end of every chapter are questions, contributed by a wise elder, Eric Norregaard, for reflection and application. They can be used individually or as part of a discussion group, and are intended to help connect the content of each chapter to your own life and context.

I have intentionally approached this as more of a practical versus theoretical book, based on true stories and testimonies from the front lines of Christian social engagement. I'm specifically writing this for all of us who are out there *doing* (or want to be) and not just discussing or debating.

Theory is important and has its place. But others have already written excellent books that delve more deeply than I do into some of the theology and ethics.[4] God made me more of an in-motion person, so this is more of an in-motion book.

In writing this I'm making the following assumptions and accepting the accompanying limitations.

1. I'm focusing on the pursuit of social justice, which is often referred to as activism or advocacy. You don't have to consider yourself a vocational activist to be engaged in social justice. Don't let the terms be intimidating or off-putting. Pursuing justice is an integral part of what it means to follow Christ. For the purpose of this book I'm defining and distinguishing between the key terms as follows:

- *Social concern/social action:* broad terms that encompass our awareness of and engagement in society, through both charity and justice.

- *Charity:* acts of mercy that help address the symptoms of problems but aren't meant to reform the underlying causes.

- *Social justice:* righting social wrongs and eradicating social inequities with the goal of creating a just society. Social justice targets broken or missing structures and systems that cause suffering and oppression.

- *Activism:* the active and intentional pursuit—including any approach, strategies or tactics—of social action in general and social justice in particular.

- *Advocacy:* speaking out on behalf of people or a cause, and promoting specific social reforms, programs, policies and the like. Advocacy is an integral part of activism.

2. I'm coming from the perspective of the millennial generation, with a generously evangelical worldview and within a broadly American cultural context. That said, I'm biracial and was born and raised in Asia until my teenage years. As a third-culture kid, I tend to process things from more of a global or crosscultural perspective.

3. There are distinct schools of thought on Christian social, cultural and political engagement coming out of the various Christian traditions. Other authors have done excellent work comparing and analyzing these approaches, and I will not be doing that here.[5]

4. I'm writing first to my fellow Christians, especially to those who are passionate about social justice but are discouraged and disillusioned by our track record in the United States and around the world. However, while this is a plainly Christian book, I hope that it also remains accessible to readers beyond the faith.

5. Finally, much of what I write comes from the experiences and lessons I've accumulated over the last ten years while I've been actively working on justice issues. Particularly, I've been heavily involved in creation-care efforts, and, while some of the stories in this book come from that work, the lessons apply more broadly to other issues as well. In each case, I've done my best to remember and acknowledge specific sources when possible. I've also used discernment in changing the details of certain individuals in order to protect their identity.

PRESSING ON

Dietrich Bonhoeffer, the German theologian and activist martyred by the Nazis, is credited with saying that "Silence in the face of evil is itself evil: God will not hold us guiltless. Not to speak is to speak. Not to act is to act."[6]

Jesus calls us to be salt and light as we reflect his image and seek his justice in a groaning world. The question is not whether we should take a stand but how we can be faithful and persevere as we do.

These are challenging days, but these are also hopeful days. And I remain greatly encouraged. Not because our struggle with injustice, evil and sin is over—it isn't—but because I've seen God working in the midst of it all, and I've experienced the healing and transformation that he can bring in us and in the world when we are faithful to him. Onward.

FOR REFLECTION AND APPLICATION

1. If you are reading this as a small group, take some time to introduce yourself. Briefly share about any interest or involvement you've had in social action. If you are reading this alone, take a moment to remind yourself why you care about injustice and how you first got involved. Where did that initial motivation come from?

2. The author mentions seeing "many well-intentioned and once-passionate Christ followers lose steam and become distracted, disengaged or in despair." Does this resonate with you? In what specific way(s) has this been true of you in the past—or right now?

3. Jesus says, "No one can serve two masters. Either you will hate the one and love the other, or you will be devoted to the one and despise the other. You cannot serve both God and money. . . . But seek first his kingdom and his righteousness, and all these things will be given to you as well" (Matthew 6:24, 33). In the surrounding verses, four things are mentioned that commonly displace God in our lives: money, food, drink and clothes. What are the things in your life that distract you from God the most, and why do you think that's the case?

4. In what way(s) are you and those around you struggling with pursuing faithfulness over effectiveness? Who do you have in your corner (besides God) reminding you to prioritize faithfulness?

5. Either in your small group or alone spend time praying this psalm.

> I remain confident of this:
>> I will see the goodness of the Lord
>> in the land of the living.
> Wait for the Lord;
>> be strong and take heart
>> and wait for the Lord. (Psalm 27:13-14)

2

IS SOCIAL ACTION NECESSARY?

Learn to do right; seek justice.
Defend the oppressed.
Take up the cause of the fatherless;
plead the case of the widow.

ISAIAH 1:17

A LOCAL REPORTER SAT IN THE FRONT ROW vigorously jotting down notes as I addressed the audience of students, faculty and community members. I was in Abilene, Texas, speaking on a couple college campuses as part of a weeklong focus on justice issues. Upon arriving, my hosts had cautioned me that social justice can be a controversial idea in this area.

When it came time for questions the reporter was the first to raise her hand. "Recently," she began, "well-known TV and radio personality Glenn Beck advised his viewers on Fox News to run as fast as they could away from any church where the words *social justice* were spoken, because he believes that they are code words for communism and Nazism. My question is how would you respond to him?"

It can be hard to anticipate what a reporter is going to ask. And I have to be careful because, when I'm feeling tired and punchy, as I was that afternoon, it's also hard to anticipate what I might say in response.

"Well," I impulsively retorted, "I would simply go out of my way *not* to interact with Glenn Beck in the first place."

Oh great, I winced inwardly, *way to get snarky on the first question!*

Thankfully, the students in the room seemed to think this was pretty funny. Their laughter gave me a chance to let my brain catch up with my mouth. "But on a more sincere note," I continued, "I would ask Mr. Beck where he found that in the Bible. Because when I read the Bible I repeatedly learn of God's passion for justice and righteousness."

Gratefully, when the article was published, she left out my initial snarky response and only printed the second part.

Glenn Beck aside, however, it's fair to say that many Christians are unsure what to think about social justice, activism and advocacy.

My work at Young Evangelicals for Climate Action (YECA)—a national initiative under the umbrella of the Evangelical Environmental Network—takes me to college campuses across the country, ranging from Penn State (Pennsylvania) to Taylor University (Indiana), and from Oral Roberts University (Oklahoma) to Samford University (Alabama), to speak about climate disruption. Along the way I find that I'm spending less time explaining why it's important to care about issues like climate change and more time discussing why we need to respond with social action.

I distinctly recall talking to a group of students at a college in the Midwest who cared deeply about peace and justice issues, and were pursuing very intentional lifestyles that would put most of us to shame. They were living in community, practicing simplicity, composting their kitchen waste, cultivating a vegetable garden, buying fair trade products and the list goes on. I was blown away by everything they were doing. As I started to share about the activism and advocacy that we pursue at YECA, however, I noticed a growing discomfort in the group. Finally, one of them spoke up, "We get that we should care about the climate crisis, but why do you put so much emphasis on activism and advocacy? Why can't we just focus on making changes in our own lives? Is social action really necessary?"

WHY WE NEED SOCIAL ACTION

Is social action really necessary? This question usually reflects a certain loss of idealism and a growing weariness, cynicism and disillusionment with the world and the role of Christians in it.

The more I get this question, however, the more I realize that two questions are being asked here. The obvious one is whether social action is *necessary*. Underneath that, however, seems to lie the related question of whether social action is *worth it*.

There are a number of challenges that give rise to these questions, but none are worth giving up over. The rest of this chapter will consider three reasons why social action really is *necessary* and then three reasons why it is also very much *worth it*.

Why social action is necessary. 1. Caring is not enough. There's a good deal of *concern* being expressed about the problems we face, but it's often manifested by a lot of talk and too little action. Being concerned is certainly an important step ahead of simply being apathetic—and there's too much selfish indifference floating around these days—but it still falls far short of the faithful response we're called to.

On one of my speaking trips I visited a prominent seminary that has an active social justice club. It was a great group, but they were few in number and had trouble gaining traction from other classmates. Their leader put it this way: "It's not so much that we don't understand justice issues and social concerns here, but that most of our campus is indifferent to doing anything to address them. There's tremendous head knowledge but it doesn't translate into much action."

On another occasion I came across a very eloquent and strongly worded article calling out the American church for doing a horrible job in caring for creation and admonishing us to ramp up our efforts. Written by a fellow Christian, the article was generally fair in its assessment, although there was little awareness of or recognition for the meaningful creation care projects being championed by an increasing number of significant ministries throughout the years. The kicker, however, was that when some of my colleagues reached out to connect with the author, she really didn't seem interested in getting involved in any of the environmental efforts herself.

There's no shortage of sentiment, posturing and opinions. That's the easy part. But such talk is vain unless it's also backed up with action. If faith without works is dead (James 2:17), then ideas are only powerful to the extent that they are lived into reality.

Being part of an entitled generation, as many of us are, we can be quick to complain and blame, and slow to take responsibility for resolving problems and fixing broken situations. This is somewhat understandable. On one hand it's relatively easy to tweet a complaint, post a critical Facebook status or even write an indignant blog about a particular injustice we've become aware of. And then stop there. This habit has become so prevalent that there's now a term for it: *slacktivism*. On the other hand it's much harder to take responsibility for actually doing something constructive to address a given problem.

Taking responsibility, however, is an integral part of what it means to be created in the image of God. True concern leads not only to more talk but also to greater action.

2. Individual action is not enough. It's important to move from sentiment to action, but not all action is created equal. The big and complicated problems we're facing today require robust and complex solutions.

Take climate disruption for example. We now know that human activity since the industrial revolution is significantly altering the chemical composition of the atmosphere and the oceans. (The oceans, vast though they may be, are now over 25 percent more acidic than pre-industrial levels due to increases in carbon pollution.) Consequently, the global climate has been changing in disruptive and mostly damaging ways, resulting in a growing ecological and humanitarian crisis. This is pretty radical and alarming stuff.

When faced with a problem of such magnitude, it's not enough for each of us to simply recycle or switch our light bulbs to energy-efficient models. I recycle and have changed all my light bulbs. I also drive a fuel-efficient car, ride my bike when possible, bring reusable bags to the grocery store, eat less meat, carry a reusable water bottle and so on. Many of us are taking individual steps such as these. And yet the planet continues to overheat, and extreme weather episodes continue to get more freakish and frequent. Solving this problem is clearly going to require action on a scale that is far greater than each of us as private individuals.

To be clear, individual lifestyle changes are always important and integral to living with integrity. These steps also do make a difference, even if it's a relatively small one. And, yes, individual actions add up as more and more of us take them.

But we can't stop there.

In order to respond faithfully to something like the climate crisis, modern-day slavery, nuclear proliferation, global hunger, failing education systems or practically any of the interconnected social and environmental problems we face, we need to take action at every level, including the policy level. In addition to individual action, we need to engage in community activism, political advocacy and even international cooperation. We need new programs, new laws, new treaties, new markets and more. In other words, our individual action must also be accompanied by social or collective action. As veteran activist Tyler Wigg-Stevenson puts it, "Actions I take as an individual, though meaningful and intrinsically worthwhile on a personal level, are meaningless to the system of injustice *unless* they are channeled strategically through a strategy of collective action."[1]

I first experienced the importance of systemic (structural or institutional) change while serving as a student representative on the sustainability committee at my college. One of our goals was to reduce the massive amounts of food waste in the campus cafeteria. Our award-winning food service provider, Bon Appétit, was part of our committee and had made great progress reducing their pre-consumption food waste. But the dining hall was operated as an all-you-can-eat buffet, and loads of food were left half-eaten on plates and trays at every meal. Bon Appétit tried raising awareness around this problem by occasionally setting out bins with all the waste collected from a previous meal. This grossed people out, but otherwise didn't lead to significant change.

So, after considerable debate, and not until a few years after I had graduated, Bon Appétit partnered with student government to introduce "Trayless Tuesdays," when trays would be removed from the dining hall. Time and again campuses have found that trays encourage guests to pile up multiple dishes and more food then they can possibly eat. Our eyes are often bigger than our stomachs. In this case Bon Appétit determined that "tray waste" came to around six hundred pounds of discarded food at every meal. When trays were not used, however, the results were dramatic:

> On the breakfast shift alone one Tuesday, lead dishwasher Fred McCarthy asked [General Manager] Raul if fewer people had come through at breakfast. He said he usually sees three to four full bags of garbage per shift, but he held up a half-full garbage bag to show Raul all that was collected.[2]

This isn't just good environmental stewardship, it's also good financial stewardship. But it didn't happen until Bon Appétit and the college worked together to make systemic improvements to the dining process. In doing so they've made far more progress in reducing food waste than any of them could have achieved individually. Maybe next they'll follow the lead of many other campuses and remove the trays altogether.

3. Charity is not enough. Social action can be broadly distinguished into two categories: charity and justice.

At the risk of oversimplifying things, charity tends to focus on alleviating the symptoms of a problem, while justice is more about dealing with the root causes. In particular, social justice seeks to fix systemic or structural wrongs by reforming a broken status quo. The goal is not equality but equity; it's not about treating everyone equally but about treating everyone rightly.

Too often today there is a tendency to emphasize charity over justice when we engage in social action. The problem is that overcoming injustice requires more than charity. Broken systems and structures hurt people and need to be fixed for the pain to stop. It's like using painkillers to treat a toothache—they may reduce the pain for a time, but it will ultimately never go away until the cavity is filled, and delaying a visit to the dentist will only make the problem worse. Perhaps the following analogy can help illuminate this blind spot.

Imagine you're sailing across the ocean on a large passenger ship that starts taking on water through leaks in the hull. Having a middle- or first-class ticket, you're on one of the upper decks of the ship and are still dry. Those stuck on the lower decks, however, are getting swamped. They frantically cry out for help. Growing concerned for their well-being, those around you throw down life preservers to keep them afloat.

Life preservers are necessary and helpful to an extent, but they don't address the underlying problem, which is that the structure of the ship needs to be fixed so that it stops taking on water. And while most of those on the upper decks remain dry so far, they're still part of a sinking ship and it's only a matter of time before they go down too.

In this case, charity is about handing out life preservers, while justice is focused on patching up the leaks. We need both.

Furthermore, while we may not always realize it, many of us live highly privileged and insulated lives, particularly from a global perspective. We're on the upper decks of society and are greatly sheltered from the injustices caused by our corrupt and broken structures. This makes it harder to recognize systemic problems when they occur. Yet just as sin has infected and corrupted us as individuals, so it has also infected and corrupted our social structures. Should we be surprised that the systems created by broken people like us are themselves flawed and open to abuse?

When we see people struggling, however, many of us tend not to blame the broken system as much as we blame the people themselves or their "unfortunate" situation. So instead of trying to fix the system, we too often focus all our efforts on charity. After all, we're used to charity—we probably come from families and churches that are involved in one way or another with clothing drives, soup kitchens, homeless shelters, canned food collections and the like.

Not only is charity more familiar but it also *seems* relatively safe, simple and palatable. Seeking justice, on the other hand, is a messy, long and complex pursuit that is often controversial and considered subversive by those invested in the status quo, which can include us. As Dom Hélder Câmara, a Brazilian archbishop from 1964 to 1985, famously stated: "When I give food to the poor, they call me a saint. When I ask why they are poor, they call me a communist."[3]

The fear of being controversial or subversive can be especially hard for those of us who were raised in churches and cultures that emphasize compliance and submission to tradition and authority. But we follow a Savior who was obedient to God and as a result was considered dangerous and subversive by the rulers of his time. And doesn't he remain just as radical by most of our standards today?

We don't always like to admit it, but engaging in charity often lets us feel good about ourselves, whereas pursuing justice can make us feel guilty as we uncover the ways our own lifestyles are complicit in the underlying problems. Activism involves challenging the status quo, and the more entrenched and comfortable we are, the more reluctant we may be to shake things up. Though it's selfish and shortsighted, sometimes we avoid seeking justice for others because we fear it will inconvenience our own lives and cost us things that we're not yet ready to surrender.

Of course, in reality, charity is not as simple or as easy as we often make it out to be. I live in a diverse low-income neighborhood that receives a lot of charity, and I've seen the great good along with the inadvertent complications—such as dependency and disempowerment—that can build up over time.

And at the end of the day charity and justice go hand in hand, and pursuing one without the other will only do so much good. A heartbreaking example of this comes out of the Second Sudanese Civil War (1983–2005).

Some of my current neighbors are refugees from what is now South Sudan, and they tell dark stories about the slave trade that flourished during the decades-long civil war, when armed militias financed their activities by regularly raiding villages and kidnapping thousands of civilians to be sold into slavery.

In a noble attempt to respond to this horrific slave trade, well-intentioned charities sprang up with the mission of buying back slaves and returning them to their families. This strategy backfired, however, as the influx of foreign financing made slavery all the more profitable and lucrative. It created a perverse incentive that increased the demand for slaves and inflated trading prices, which made it even harder for villagers to redeem their family members.

Many organizations, including UNICEF and the United Nations, criticized these charitable efforts as causing more harm than good. The Sudan Council of Churches and New Sudan Council of Churches—representing both Catholic and Protestants—released a statement saying that despite the good intentions of slave redemption, slavery would only end when the greater crises in Sudan was resolved. And in the end many of those liberated by the charities were tragically recaptured by the militias and trafficked all over again.

It's easy to criticize those behind the slave redemption efforts, but what would you do in such a situation? Wouldn't we all be compelled to do everything in our power to save someone from a life of slavery, even if it meant buying back their freedom?

We are called to practice sacrificial charity, and charity done well is a force for great good. But, as the Sudanese slave trade demonstrated, charity has limitations and ultimately cannot succeed without justice. This isn't a new idea. You can barely turn a page in the Old Testament Prophets without hearing God blast Israel for their lack of compassion toward the poor *and* for their broken systems that caused such poverty (see for example Isaiah 10:1-3; 58; Amos 5:11-12; 8:4-7; Micah 2:1-3; Malachi 3:5). And throughout the Scriptures, God repeatedly and unequivocally exhorts his people to pursue both charity and justice:

He has shown you, O mortal, what is good.
    And what does the LORD require of you?
To act justly and to love mercy
    and to walk humbly with your God. (Micah 6:8)

Bringing it all together. When my good friend and neighbor Matthew Soerens graduated from college, he found an entry-level job working in the Immigrant Legal Services department at a local branch of World Relief, the relief-and-development arm of the National Association of Evangelicals. In this role Matt was trained to help immigrants and refugees navigate the US immigration and naturalization system.

The more time he spent at World Relief, however, the more his heart grew for his clients and the struggles they faced in transitioning to America and trying to provide for their families. He wanted to do more than get to know them during office hours. So Matt ended up moving into one of the neighborhoods that World Relief resettles refugees in.

Over time, rich relationships blossomed between Matt and his neighbors. He would help them with any questions or needs that he could address and, meanwhile, they would bring him good home-cooked meals, which he never turned down.

His work combined with his living situation helped him see firsthand just how broken our immigration system had become and how much it needed reform. So he started to take the next step, from focusing on charity efforts to engaging in activism and advocacy.

In time he ended up coauthoring one of the definitive books on immigration reform from a Christian perspective, titled *Welcoming the Stranger*.[4] There wasn't much of a Christian immigration reform movement at that time, so, with World Relief's support, he transitioned into a new role centered on church engagement, and worked with others to build the movement from the ground up.

Through Matt's faithful work and example, many Christians from all walks of life and all parts of America have become aware of and found their own ways to get involved in loving their immigrant neighbors and advocating for comprehensive immigration reform. What an encouraging example of what it can look like for us to actively address injustice through charity and justice at both the individual and collective levels.

Matt's journey didn't happen overnight and is not necessarily typical of what to expect when we engage in an issue. Things will look different for each of us, but, like Matt, we start where God has placed us, and then keep following step by step wherever he leads.

Is social action worth it? "Is social action really *necessary*?" The chapter began with this question and went on to address three reasons why we need it. But what about the often underlying question of whether social action—and social justice in particular—is really *worth it*?

Pursuing justice is risky, and just like any other aspect of following Jesus, it comes at a cost, especially to what worldly comfort, stability and security we have in our grasp. Is it worth the time and the tears? Is it worth the sweat and the struggle? Is it worth the opposition and, yes, at times even the bloodshed? At the end of the day, is social action worth the cost?

The longer I do this work, the more I believe that it is.

1. Social action is worth it to us. The more we keep Jesus at the center then the more worthwhile social action becomes. Social action aligns us with God's kingdom instead of with the broken status quo— with the way the world should be, not just the way it is now. It stretches us, which leads to growth, and challenges us to live more fully and love more deeply. It empowers us to exercise our human calling to be responsible and compassionate stewards of the earth and each other. And it leads us to take up our cross and follow after Christ daily. And every step closer in our walk with Christ is always worth the cost. As Jim Elliot, the martyred missionary to the Huaorani, famously wrote: "He is no fool who gives what he cannot keep to gain that which he cannot lose."[5]

One of the members of the intentional community I live in—we'll call her Natalie—currently works in the corporate world. Her colleagues cannot fathom why she lives with us in a low-income apartment complex when she gets paid enough to live somewhere much nicer. The culture in their office puts a high value on things like trendy clothes and expensive cars. Natalie often feels drawn to such luxury and struggles with the temptation to pursue a lifestyle of conspicuous consumption. She tells me that living in our neighborhood and seeking the welfare of our neighbors, both through service and activism, helps keep her grounded as she works in corporate America.

2. *Social action is also worth it to* our neighbors. In a world where over two billion people still live on less than two dollars a day, most of us lead unbelievably privileged and insulated lives.[6] If we are serious about obeying the great command to love our neighbors, then our social action is just as much for their benefit as it is for our own. They are the ones suffering most directly from the impacts of the injustice and oppression we're all striving to overcome.

Social action is worth it to my undocumented neighbor who longs for our immigration system to be reformed so she can get right with the law without being put in jail and separated from her family.

It's worth it to the kids from the low-income Chicago neighborhood I used to live in, who are growing up next to a dirty coal-fired power plant that was finally forced to clean up its disease-causing pollution or else shut down.

It's worth it to the thousands of modern-day slaves who are liberated every year by partnerships between law enforcement and nonprofits such as International Justice Mission.

It's worth it to those who are marginalized—which still include far too many women and minorities—who deserve to be more fairly treated and who long to more fully share in the rights and opportunities that those with power often take for granted.

For as long as there is evil, brokenness and injustice in our world, social action will always be worth it and will always be called for.

3. *Social action is also worth it to* God. The ultimate reason we pursue social action isn't just because it's worth it to us or even to our neighbors, but because it's worth it to *God*, the Father of the fatherless, the helper of the widows, the protector of the outsiders and the provider for the poor. If it's worth it to God, it will always be worth it to us.

FOR REFLECTION AND APPLICATION

1. When you talk with others about social action, what kind of response do you get? Bored indifference? Enthusiasm that never seems to translate into action? Encouragement? Anger? Why do you think this is the case?

2. In a hyperindividualistic society, we applaud the one man who covers his roof with solar panels or the one woman who generates zero waste, but this chapter argues that those individual actions are relatively meaningless unless they translate into collective action. Can you think of an example where one person's action was more powerful than an entire movement?

3. Where would you say your church puts its emphasis: on charity or social justice? Why do you think that's true?

4. The prophets in Scripture called for both charity and social justice. Take a look at Isaiah 58 and note that it calls for small personal acts of compassion as well as the large-scale overhaul of an unjust system. How can this passage help inform our worship and church life today?

5. Which part of this verse is most challenging to how you live your
   life?

> He has shown you, O mortal, what is good.
>   And what does the LORD require of you?
> To act justly and to love mercy
>   and to walk humbly with your God. (Micah 6:8)

3

OVERCOMING OBSTACLES
TO SOCIAL ACTION

Do not conform to the pattern of this world,
but be transformed by the renewing of your mind.
Then you will be able to test and approve what God's
will is—his good, pleasing and perfect will.

ROMANS 12:2

I'M NEVER MORE PERSUASIVE than when trying to avoid something I really don't want to do.

The hardest thing I've ever done so far as an activist is run for US Congress. And I tried spiritedly to rationalize myself out of doing it.

In 2010 there was an unexpected opening in the congressional district where I live—no one was stepping up to run against the incumbent. Though a fellow Christian, I found his record on poverty alleviation, environmental stewardship, immigration reform and other issues to be largely disappointing. Beyond his policies I was also increasingly disillusioned by his politics and the fear-based attack ads targeting his opponents that ran during election years.

Upon hearing that no one was challenging him in either the primary or general election, a group of us in the district started looking on both sides of the aisle for the right person to step up. We were eager to seize this rare opportunity to run a different kind of race and create an alternative to the political status quo that we were well fed up with.

It was a race against time and as one by one our obvious choices all declined, my friends and colleagues started asking me to consider running. Things were obviously getting desperate!

An Unlikely Candidate

There are many good reasons *not* to run for political office, and I certainly wasn't an obvious candidate.

Running for Congress can be an overwhelmingly stressful and expensive endeavor. Having just turned twenty-five, which happens to be the legal age cutoff for serving in the House of Representatives, I was woefully inexperienced and underfunded. I didn't want to quit my very meaningful job in order to campaign, I had only a modest amount of hard-earned money saved up in my bank account, and I had never before been directly involved in political parties or campaigns.

On top of all this, I'm an introvert and there are few things I dislike more than conflict and competition. When I get worn out, my face often develops an involuntary twitch, which is not so great during hours of public speaking and interaction. Growing up, my concerned father encouraged me to pursue a relatively quiet and stable career. Like accounting, perhaps. But certainly not electoral politics.

So, there were a lot of reasons why running for Congress could be a bad idea for me. But there were also good reasons *to run* for Congress.

Here was an opportunity to fight for key issues, such as immigration reform and environmental stewardship, and to speak up for the poor and marginalized in our community. Their rights and needs are both real and urgent, but their voices often go unheard in political deliberations. As influential pastor Tim Keller observes, "Our political and economic systems do not listen to people without money and other forms of social power."[1]

Here also was an opportunity to move from simply complaining to actually taking responsibility and, in the words of Gandhi, become the change I longed to see. By running perhaps I could help create some space for political orphans like myself to engage in a renewed politics and Christian public witness, one characterized more by faithfulness than by worldly measures of success. Besides, if I did not step up now, we might never have another chance at such an opportunity.

I had promised to seriously consider the opportunity, and the more I prayed about it, the more I realized that my reasons for turning down this challenge sounded rational on the surface, but deeper down were largely motivated by fear and insecurity. I realized that walking away might be the *safe* thing to do, but I did not believe in this case that it was the *right* thing to do. And that's quite simply what it came down to: at the end of the day I decided, in community and to the best of my understanding, that running for Congress appeared to be the right thing to do.

And so began an unforgettable journey into grassroots campaigning and advocacy that I'll share about further in the chapters ahead. It was more painful and stretching than I could have imagined, and there were nights when I would wake up from campaign-related nightmares drenched in a cold sweat. Nonetheless, it was also immensely rewarding. I will always be glad that I agreed to do it, and I'm so grateful that God gave me the strength I continuously prayed for in order to make it through.

Whether it was making the decision to run for Congress or any of the other hard choices I've struggled with and continue to face, I've found wisdom in the saying that if it's a worthwhile endeavor, then it's probably going to be hard.

In the same way, there are usually many reasons for any of us to avoid engaging in social action. Some are simply lame excuses motivated by apathy, but others are sincere concerns borne out of experience and observation. Being faithful involves taking these into consideration and then prayerfully determining and choosing the right path forward. The rest of this chapter focuses more in-depth on three common reasons for eschewing social action and how we can overcome them.

STRUGGLE ONE: IT'S TOO OVERWHELMING

It's easy to become paralyzed by the amount of need in the world.

Every day the news is filled with new tragedies both at home and abroad: shootings, gang rapes, terrorist attacks, civil wars, disease outbreaks, highway pileups, industrial accidents, monster tornados, devastating floods and earthquakes, and so much more. As Tyler Wigg-Stevenson notes, "Massive suffering is nothing new, but real-time global knowledge of it is."[2]

With updates on everything streaming in all the time from everywhere—through both traditional news sources and social media—we're incessantly bombarded with images and stories of evil, injustice and suffering. And thanks to our smartphones, tablets and other gadgets, we now no longer need to get out of bed in the morning before we're connected to and subsequently overwhelmed by current events.

But many of us don't even need the news in order to come face to face with unending need. All I have to do is walk around in the low-income apartment complex where I live and I'm faced with poverty, unemployment, alcoholism, mental and physical illness, and all manner of struggles. Any neighborhood has its share of these problems—many wealthy suburban areas are plagued by depression, eating disorders and prescription drug abuse—although in most communities they're often carefully hidden.

So where's the balance? How can we stay informed and engaged without becoming overwhelmed and numbed by all the need surrounding us?

It's never easy. The key, however, is to begin responding not to need but to calling. Greg Carmer, dean of the chapel at Gordon College, expounds on this principle: "A mature understanding of the unity of the body of Christ allows us to care about everything Christ cares about, but to carry only what he has given us to bear."[3]

Calling is connected to but not defined by need. Frederick Buechner puts it this way: "The place God calls you to is the place where your deep gladness and the world's deep hunger meet."[4]

It's the "Nehemiah Principle," which my good friend Tom Rowley, who heads up A Rocha USA, first introduced me to when explaining A Rocha's philosophy of nurturing a network of local community-based conservation projects.

Upon realizing both the need and opportunity to rebuild Jerusalem, Nehemiah knew not to shoulder the task on his own. Instead, he empowered each individual family to rebuild the city through their own unique contributions and in their own respective places. One section at a time; one calling at a time.

In the end it was this powerful unity and God's intervention that protected the city. Like Nehemiah's band of Israelites, the church is a body working together to carry out the mission of God: "For just as each of us has one body with many members, and these members do not all have the same function, so in Christ we, though many, form one body, and each member belongs to all the others" (Romans 12:4-5).

Responding solely to need is a temptation to take matters into our own hands, which is a recipe for fatigue. Pursuing our calling, on the other hand, aligns us with God's will, submits us to his timing and avails us of his provision.

Most of us won't be called to run for Congress, for instance, but there are many other ways that each of us may be called to engage our political process and system. As veteran organizers Alexia Salvatierra and Peter Heltzel note,

> Romans 13 teaches that governments have a divine purpose to ensure the wellbeing of their society. And in the Hebrew Scrip-

tures, the King is often exhorted to ensure justice for the poor
and to care for the widow, the orphan and the stranger. . . . In a
monarchy, the king has the power and responsibility to ensure
this command. In a democracy, we all have the power—and the
corresponding responsibility.[5]

We steward this gift and responsibility by becoming informed
voters, by supporting candidates from any party who have integrity
and similar values, by communicating with our elected officials on key
issues, by writing letters to the editor and speaking thoughtfully on
things that matter to us, by serving as an appointee on a commission
or even by working in an administration. The opportunities are
endless. And for those who *are* called to run for elected office and
influence the system from the inside out, there are many different
ways to serve—from student government to the school board and
from the city council to state and federal government.

Finally, what's true of our political engagement also extends to the
rest of our Christian discipleship and witness, no matter what the
issue. We are not called to save the world, but we follow the God who
is, and who invites us to be a meaningful part of his great and unstop-
pable mission. As Duane Litfin, the former president of Wheaton
College, often says, "You can't do everything, but you can do something. What is the something that God is calling you to do?"[6]

STRUGGLE TWO: IT'S TOO CONTROVERSIAL

Another common reason for avoiding social action is that it's too complicated and controversial.

Causes may start out relatively straightforward—everyone is for
good education, low unemployment, fair immigration laws and
clean air—but things get messy quickly as high-level principles are
worked into ground level policies, projects and programs. How do
we prioritize our ideals and goals? How do we go about pursuing
them and who is responsible? What's the role of the government

versus the church versus the individual? Where is the money going to come from? And the questions just keep coming.

In polarizing times such as ours, it can be hard to know which side, if any, is right on a given issue. Life is hectic and there are only so many things that we can invest the time and energy to understand in depth. Everything else is much easier to simply not have a position on. After all, how many of us enjoy getting caught up in controversy?

Controversy creates confusion, and this makes it risky to take a stand on something we don't have all the answers to. A close friend who I had been repeatedly trying to recruit for a social justice campaign finally sat me down one day and explained that she didn't feel confident enough to be of much help. She supported us, but was still very hesitant to get visibly or vocally involved out of concern that, because the issues were so messy and there was a lot she didn't understand, she would inadvertently end up looking like a fool and doing the cause more harm than good. This is a valid and common concern, which is why good resources like Steve Corbett and Brian Fikkert's *When Helping Hurts* and Robert D. Lupton's *Toxic Charity* are so important and have been so well-received.[7]

This adverseness is especially pronounced when the focus becomes more political—such as signing a petition, asking questions at a public hearing or calling members of Congress about specific legislation. When I ran for Congress I was deeply encouraged by the many friends who responded enthusiastically and played significant roles in supporting my campaign. But I was also surprised by the number of people close to me who agreed with what I stood for but chose not to get involved because it was "too political." For them, and for many others, the process is too intimidating and our systems are too broken to be involved in.

So how do we move forward when social action gets messy like this?

The simple though not very satisfying answer is that we need to make peace with the gray areas, both in our faith and in the world. Many important issues are not always black and white, and if the solutions were as simple and uncontroversial as we'd like them to be, there's a good chance they would also have been implemented by now.

So we learn as much as we can about the issues and then find experts who we can trust in areas that are beyond our familiarity. This takes prayer and good discernment. It also takes the humility to recognize that we all have room to learn and grow, and that we may need to modify our positions as new knowledge comes in. Embracing diverse perspectives and fostering healthy dialogue helps expose our blind spots and expand our understanding.

At the end of the day we're called to do our best with the information we've been given. It's hard to see God judging us for what we have no way of knowing, but it's pretty clear that we will be held accountable for what we do know and yet don't act on.

The Evangelical Immigration Table (evangelicalimmigrationtable .com) is an encouraging example of how we can creatively engage in a complicated and often controversial issue.

Fixing the broken US immigration system has been contentious for decades in both society and the church. While everyone agrees that the system needs reform, it's far tougher to find agreement on the specifics of what the solution should look like, especially as it has to do with the millions of undocumented immigrants already trapped living in the shadows of our society.

But immigration reform is not just a complicated political issue; it's also a moral and biblical concern.[8] This is where a politically diverse group of Christian leaders have been able to transcend the partisan controversy and find common ground to work together for the common good. The Evangelical Immigration Table is a broad coalition made up of key evangelical groups—including the Southern Baptist Convention, the National Association of Evangelicals and Sojourners—who are all committed to advocating for reform.

Though the process hasn't always been easy, one of the keys behind their success is that the group includes key theologians and immigration experts who helped to identify a set of shared principles that should underlie any attempt at reform. Based on these shared core values, each group then had the space to educate their constituencies and work out where they would fall on specific policies. And, when possible, they organized joint press conferences and advocacy events to get the word out and put pressure on Congress to act.

Instead of being paralyzed by the complexity and controversy around the immigration issue, the Evangelical Immigration Table has prayerfully persevered in staking out common ground on high-level principles and in placing biblical values over partisan politics. They have sorted out the facts from the ideological hype and distinguished between what was essential, what they could negotiate on and what they should leave for each group to decide for themselves.

As a result, the Evangelical Immigration Table has accomplished far more than anyone thought possible in just a few years, and they have brought much publicity both to the immigration issue as well as to the constructive and compassionate role that Christians can play in the public square.

In the words of Martin Luther King Jr., "The ultimate measure of a [person] is not where [he or she] stands in moments of comfort and convenience, but where [he or she] stands at times of challenge and controversy."[9]

STRUGGLE THREE: IT'S TOO DIFFERENT

A final reason for avoiding social action is because we don't know or like the other people doing it. Often those already engaged on a given issue or movement are different from us and therefore hard to identify with or relate to. Perhaps they're more progressive or more conservative than we are. Or perhaps they simply come across as weird or unpleasant.

Sometimes this is a reaction to prevailing stereotypes and caricatures— whether it's of free-spirited, long-haired hippies strumming for peace or straight-laced, Bible thumpers picketing in front of abortion clinics.

But is this a legitimate reason for us not to get involved? Perhaps it's as straightforward as setting aside our discomfort and insecurity, and intentionally embracing those who seem different from us. Just like Jesus did. And as we build relationships with folks, we'll probably be surprised by how much we can relate to or affirm in each other.

I served as a youth group counselor at my local church for a number of years, and during that time we regularly addressed the problem of social cliques and how they fracture community and run counter to our calling as Christians. After all, Jesus was infamous for hanging out with all manner of people who didn't usually mingle, whether they were fishermen, Samaritans, lepers, tax collectors or religious leaders.

At the end of the day we're all human beings created in the image of God, regardless of how we each dress, talk, smell or vote. Why would we avoid advocating for peace just because we don't look like hippies? Or why would we ignore the problem of abortion just because we didn't want to come across as angry Bible thumpers?

A related but weightier consideration, however, is how to collaborate with people who have very different beliefs and values than we do. I regularly face this concern in my work on environmental issues, where I'm blessed to interact with people of diverse faiths and worldviews. Functionally, my work is about a dual apologetic: on one hand I engage the church around why and how environmental concerns are relevant to our faith; on the other hand I engage the environmental community around why and how Jesus Christ is relevant to the problems we're facing as a people and planet.

From time to time, when fellow Christians learn about my collaboration with secular groups such as the Sierra Club, the UN Foundation or the National Wildlife Federation (which, by the way, has been led for many years by Larry Schweiger, who is an outspoken evangelical Christian), they express concern over whether my faith is at risk.

As a former missionary kid, this makes little sense to me. We send missionaries all around the world to minister among people of different faiths in very challenging and even dangerous contexts. Yet somehow we're less comfortable about working with non-Christian groups in America, even when much of what they do is good work that the church should be involved in as well. And doesn't everyone need Jesus anyway?

Wherever God leads us, we always need to be careful not to lose our distinctiveness or compromise our values and integrity. Fundamentally, however, if we believe that all truth is God's truth, we have nothing and no one to fear.

At the same time, there are certain boundaries we should hold to, such as the distinction between interfaith collaboration and interfaith worship. Interfaith collaboration can be very healthy and enriching. But while we can learn a lot from each other, and while we can accomplish a lot together, it is appropriate to keep our worship distinct. Not only is this biblical but it just makes sense if we believe that the almighty God we follow is not the same as the gods that other religions worship. Interfaith worship services are increasingly popular in America today, but they are more often the fruit of civil religion than biblical faith.

LIVING IN THE KINGDOM

There are many other reasons why social action may be unappealing or inconvenient at any given time.

When we're students, it may be because we have to focus on our studies. When we're in the working world, it may be because we've got to find and keep our jobs. Those of us with families need to care and provide for them, and those who are still young may not feel ready to take on serious responsibilities. As we get older we may feel like we missed our chance to get involved, or that we're weary from fighting all our lives and just want to rest and enjoy the years that remain.

But who are we kidding? Today is always the day for justice and peace, and now is always the right time to follow God's calling. Taking seriously the commands to love God and love our neighbor inevitably leads to social action.

Margaret Philbrick and her husband, Charlie, have three kids and live in the town next to mine. Their family has sponsored a Rwandan girl through World Vision for a number of years, and through that relationship Margaret began sensing a call to get more involved in missions. For various reasons, however, she and Charlie determined that going overseas wasn't practical for their family. Disappointed, Margaret turned to prayer for God's guidance. It was around that time that she heard Parkside—the community I'm part of—needed more volunteers for our neighborhood kids ministries. After Margaret talked it over with her family, they decided to come check things out, which is how she ended up in my living room helping to lead one of our weekly children's Bible studies. The Philbricks have since become regular volunteers here, which led to them also getting involved in advocacy efforts to help protect our neighborhood from being redeveloped. Here are some of Margaret's reflections about their experience:

> Every Sunday evening, eight girls gather for Bible study, prayer, sharing our "highs and lows" from the past week and eating their favorite, chicken noodle soup. It's basic discipleship and mentoring 101. It's not a sexy ministry (i.e. evangelizing remote communities along the Amazon river), but it's good. . . . After eight months, we've grown to love these boys and girls. . . . It was as if the Lord was saying, "Sure, I'd love for you to go to Rwanda, but I need you to learn how to love these people at home first."[10]

Everyday Christians like Margaret, her family and countless others like them show us that social action is not just for a select few with some sort of formal training; it's for all of us. Try all we want, we'll always reach a point in our faith where we cannot be all that God wants us to be unless we embrace the biblical call to justice and reconciliation. The longer we resist, the more callous and entrenched we become. This doesn't negate real and healthy responsibilities to our studies, work, families and the like. But it does mean that we learn the lesson of Jonah and run toward God's calling and kingdom, not away and into our own inferior and unfaithful plans.

There are many reasons to avoid social action, but by the empowerment of the Holy Spirit all the excuses in the world are not enough to prevent us from doing what is right. Jesus has saved us from sin. His mercy, grace and forgiveness mean that we can now join him in his mission. No more do we order our lives around the wants and worries of the world; now we seek first the kingdom and God's righteousness (Matthew 6:33).

FOR REFLECTION AND APPLICATION

1. What are your own obstacles to being involved in social action?

2. If there is one area of social action you focus on, is it "the place where your deep gladness and the world's deep hunger meet"?

3. If you often feel overwhelmed, is it possible that you are trying to carry more than God has given you to carry? What burdens are you carrying?

4. The Evangelical Immigration Table is held up as an example of conservatives, moderates and progressives talking together and then advocating for reform. Have you ever been—or are you now—part of a similar group of diverse people pursuing social justice together? If so, tell your group or someone else about it. Or are all your colaborers people who think just like you?

5. Things that are obviously unjust to us may not yet be obvious to others. And we may have forgotten that there was a process by which we were transformed and our minds renewed—so that things that were once not obvious to us have now become obvious. Is there some way that you can encourage or nurture other people to "Learn to do right; seek justice. Defend the oppressed. Take up the cause of the fatherless; plead the case of the widow"? What is it?

RECONCILING EVANGELISM
AND SOCIAL ACTION

Therefore go and make disciples of all nations,
baptizing them in the name of the Father and of the Son
and of the Holy Spirit, and teaching them to obey everything
I have commanded you. And surely I am with
you always, to the very end of the age.

MATTHEW 28:19-20

ACCORDING TO THE WORLD HEALTH ORGANIZATION, an estimated 54.5 million people die every year.[1] That's roughly 150,000 deaths every day. And almost two deaths every second. In the time it took you to read this paragraph, twenty fellow humans with unique names, families and stories just took their last breaths. It's a sobering reality.

Even more sobering is that many of these deaths—thousands daily and millions annually—are preventable and directly attributable to injustice, whether drought, pollution, famine, disease, violence or a myriad of other curses. Some people pass away from natural causes after living relatively full and blessed lives. But in a world where six thousand children die every day from a lack of clean water alone, what should be the norm is still far too often the exception.[2]

In addition to all these deaths, injustice also causes tremendous hardship for the living. What about the millions of people who are currently trapped in suffering and oppression? According to International Justice Mission, more people are enslaved in human trafficking today than during the entire trans-Atlantic slave trade.[3] Over one billion people around the world scrape by in extreme poverty on less than one dollar per day, and another billion or more live on less than two dollars per day.[4] While progress continues to be made on many of these fronts, there is still much work to be done and many global health, justice and development goals remain far out of reach.

At the same time, thousands of people are also dying every day without knowing or even hearing of Jesus Christ. While Christianity has grown to include over two billion people, that statistic still excludes two-thirds of the world's population.[5] And, according to some estimates, around 40 percent of the world's population still live in unreached people groups and have little to no access to the gospel.[6] What about this grave injustice? What about the condition of those dying *as well as* living without Jesus?

Taking a step back, many Christians wonder which of the above sets of statistics is more important—should we care more about saving souls or about making this world a better place?

On Mission with God

Growing up as a missionary kid, I understood the importance of evangelism at an early age. And when I was sixteen, I experienced a personal revival during a church missions conference and my faith came alive in a fresh and powerful way.

My family had just moved back to the United States, and I came to view my new high school as a mission field. I read books on how to share my faith and posted a copy of the Great Commission (Matthew 28:18-20) on the wall above my bed. I participated enthusiastically in the after-school prayer club every week, talked to my classmates and teachers about Jesus, and found a way to tie almost all my essays in English class back to my faith. When I visited my high school several years after graduating, the first question my former history teacher asked was if I had become a preacher yet.

During my college years I grew more aware of the grave injustices and immense suffering happening in the world. Jesus calls us to love our neighbors—even our enemies—and far too many of our neighbors are hungry, thirsty, sick, homeless, oppressed and enslaved. These issues tugged at my heart. I prayed for God's kingdom to come on earth as it is in heaven, and I yearned to be part of that mission.

So I studied environmental science with an eye toward one day working overseas in sustainable development. And I spent the summer before my senior year as part of a team researching the ways that climate change is devastating local communities on the shores of Lake Tanganyika in East Africa. While collecting data on the fishing beaches I also contracted malaria and giardia, which made the importance of clean water and good healthcare all the more personal.

I was on fire for Jesus Christ and wanted my life to count for him in the greatest way possible. And this is where I was torn: Is my primary responsibility as a Christian focused on evangelism or social action?

This tension is not uncommon and certainly not new.

THE SWINGING PENDULUM

For over a hundred years, Protestants in the United States have struggled to agree on our mission in the world. The result is a largely unnecessary dichotomy between two supposedly dueling priorities: evangelism and social concern.

In the early twentieth century a dramatic split occurred between the theologically liberal mainline Protestant denominations (which espoused the social gospel and championed a social transformation model of engagement focused more on systemic and political reform), and the theologically conservative fundamentalist movement (which espoused the fundamentals of the faith and championed a personal transformation model of engagement focused more on evangelism and conversion).[7]

In other words, and at risk of considerably oversimplifying the matter, the primary mission of the church was either to save souls or improve society, and "never the twain shall meet." Sound familiar?

Modern-day evangelicalism largely came out of fundamentalism, and over time evangelicals sought to recover a more healthy social concern that had been shunned by fundamentalists coming out of the split with mainline denominations. Evidence of this evangelical recovery include Carl F. H. Henry's famous book *The Uneasy Conscience of Modern Fundamentalism*, first published in 1947, along with the *Chicago Declaration* (1973) and the *Chicago Declaration II: A Call for Evangelical Renewal* (1993).

Most notably, however, the last fifty years of evangelical and fundamentalist reengagement in the public square has been heavily focused on a narrow set of culture war issues such as abortion, sexuality and religious liberty (including creation versus evolution, prayer in public schools, public display of the Ten Commandments and so on). And while the culture wars continue to rage today, the hegemony of the religious right has weakened. Growing instead are indications that Christians are slowly but surely caring about a much more holistic range of justice concerns that include many of the issues covered in this book (more on the culture wars and our expanding social agenda in chaps. 5–6).

At the same time there remains an underlying tension within American Christianity between how much we focus on social action versus evangelism, and whether our efforts to make the world better inhibit our efforts to spread the gospel. Some have characterized this dynamic as a pendulum swinging between two competing priorities, and there is concern that many of us are in the process of swinging away from evangelism and toward the social gospel. These concerns may not be completely unfounded.

Today, as the world flattens at an exponential rate, younger generations of Christians are increasingly exposed to the realities of global poverty and injustice. Any illusion that we can faithfully follow Jesus without addressing the evil and brokenness in the world around us is fading fast.

Amen.

At the same time, however, in this postmodern and post-Christian age, claims of exclusivity are considered intolerant, and there's growing pushback on evangelism as being intrusive and inappropriate.

Largely gone is the era of Billy Graham crusades that would fill entire stadiums. In an increasingly pluralistic and relativistic society, social action appears much more appealing than evangelism. Feed the hungry and we get applause. Invite people to repentance and salvation and those cheers often turn into jeers.

Much more can be said about how we arrived at this point, and understanding our history is certainly valuable. The purpose of the rest of this chapter, however, is to explore how we can move forward by reconciling—not simply trying to balance—what should be understood as integral and complimentary parts of a holistic gospel and mission. Getting this right is key to engaging faithfully in social action today.

FALSE DICHOTOMIES

One of the most common concerns I hear about my generation (coming mainly from older evangelicals) is that we're too much about justice and too little about evangelism; we've messed up our priorities and risk losing the core of our faith.

But one of the most repeated criticisms I hear my generation level against our elders is that they focused so exclusively on evangelism that they largely neglected social justice. And when they did engage social issues it was skewed toward fighting the culture wars and selectively (often hypocritically) targeting issues of personal and sexual immorality while ignoring if not perpetuating other social and economic injustices.

The real issue here is not which side is right—in many ways they're reactions against each other—but that neither side is right on its own. Evangelism *versus* social action is a false dichotomy. These are complementary, not competing, priorities—it's both-and, not either-or. Just as you need both parts of a pair of scissors or both wings of an airplane, both personal transformation and social transformation are desperately needed. Neither can stand alone, and, not surprisingly, problems arise when we pit one integral part of the gospel against another.

On one hand, the problem with only emphasizing evangelism is that we narrow the gospel down to how it benefits individual souls to the neglect of most everything else that is broken, whether it's our social structures or the rest of God's creation. We make Jesus out to be only partially successful in his mission to overthrow sin as "far as the curse is found"—which is everywhere, not just in our souls. What happens to everything else that groans under the weight of sin? Is God in some way cutting his losses and giving up on it all? And if he's not, then why would we?

On the other hand, the problem with only emphasizing social action is that we take a naive and shallow approach to the problem of sin. All of the interconnected crises we face today—whether hunger, genocide, poverty or climate disruption—are not just technical problems with political, programmatic or technological solutions. At a deeper level they're moral problems caused by vices such as greed, apathy, pride and selfishness. To put it more precisely, the root of all our interconnected crises is the problem of sin. And so what we ultimately need is a solution to sin.

I spoke at a Christian college recently where some students challenged me for focusing in on the problem of sin because it's not winsome or inclusive. To the contrary, they argued, it can be offensive and exclusive, especially to those who do not believe in Jesus. I agree that sin is a hard topic, and there are few things I like less than potentially being offensive or exclusive. But admitting that we have a problem is the first step to addressing it. Call it whatever we like—evil, depravity, immorality, brokenness—how can we ignore the underlying pervasiveness of sin in ourselves and in the world, even regardless of what we believe about God? How can we hope to fix our other problems apart from having a solution to this root cause? And do any of us really believe that we can heal ourselves of all our brokenness?

The reality is that we can't introduce people to Jesus while ignoring the problems in the world, and we can't try to fix the world while ignoring that the only true answer comes through Christ. Evangelism and social concern are integrally connected; faithful social action involves reconciling these priorities back to a biblically holistic approach.

A HOLISTIC MISSION

At its best the Christian faith has always been about striving to understand, live and proclaim a holistic gospel and mission. The Lausanne Movement is a prime example.

In July 1974 over 2,500 Christian leaders from over 150 countries met in Lausanne, Switzerland, in a unprecedented conference that launched the Lausanne Covenant and, shortly after, the Lausanne Committee for World Evangelization. Convened by renowned evangelist Billy Graham, the purpose of this gathering was to "unite all evangelicals in the common task of the total evangelization of the world."[8]

John Stott, a respected British pastor and Bible expositor, became the chief architect responsible for drafting the Lausanne Covenant, and this is where some controversy arose. Graham and others wanted Lausanne to focus on evangelism and evangelistic missions, but Stott believed that they should address both evangelism and social action: "If we love our neighbors as God created them (which is God's command to us), then we shall inevitably be concerned for their total welfare, the welfare of their bodies, their souls, and their society."[9]

In the end a more balanced approach prevailed and eventually solidified into the motto that the Lausanne Movement still uses today: "The whole church taking the whole gospel to the whole world."

Reflecting on John Stott's ministry, Rowan Williams, the former

Archbishop of Canterbury, noted, "It is not too much to say that he helped to change the face of evangelicalism internationally, arguing for the necessity of 'holistic' mission that applied the gospel of Jesus to every area of life, including social and political questions."[10]

John Stott passed away in 2011, but his legacy of championing both evangelism and social action continues on in the Lausanne Movement, which now designates senior associates on topics ranging from creation care and children at risk to disability concerns and anticorruption.

The Third Lausanne Congress on World Evangelization, held in Cape Town, South Africa, in 2010 (Lausanne II was held in Manila in 1989), brought together a record-breaking four thousand leaders from 198 countries, along with thousands more remote participants, in what *Christianity Today* called "the most representative gathering of Christian leaders in history."[11] It resulted in the release of the "Cape Town Commitment"—a robust evangelical manifesto that renews the original Lausanne Covenant and clearly lays out a holistic gospel and mission in two parts titled "For the Lord We Love" and "For the World We Serve" respectively.

Here's an excerpt from the "Cape Town Commitment" that is helpful for understanding and articulating how evangelism and social action belong together:

> Integral mission means discerning, proclaiming, and living out the biblical truth that the gospel is God's good news, through the cross and resurrection of Jesus Christ, for individual persons, and for society, and for creation. All three are broken and suffering because of sin; all three are included in the redeeming love and mission of God; all three must be part of the comprehensive mission of God's people.[12]

Al Hsu, my editor at InterVarsity Press, was present at Cape Town 2010 and later commented that it seems "the evangelism-only prioritization is a luxury of the privileged West where poverty, war, genocide or famine is not as visible or can be more easily ignored.

For most of the world, if the gospel doesn't speak to social realities and injustices, it's irrelevant and has nothing to say."[13]

There's a deep hunger in the world today, not merely for an explanation of the existence of evil and injustice, but for a true and lasting solution to it. The gospel is the supremely good news that Christ has made a way, and it is done. Through his death and resurrection, Jesus has defeated the powers of sin and evil, has established the kingdom of God and is reconciling all things to himself (Col 1:15-20). All things. Everything that was lost and broken because of our sin is to be rescued and will one day be restored to its original, God-intended state of shalom.

And, in the meantime, God calls us to be his witnesses to the ends of the earth. We are to proclaim and live out the truth that Christ has triumphed over all sin and suffering and death. Jesus is the true hope of the planet, and he invites us to be both the recipients and agents of this reconciliation, participating in the coming of his kingdom here on earth as it is in heaven.

So what can it look like to live out a holistic gospel and mission?

A MINISTRY EXAMPLE: INTERVARSITY CHRISTIAN FELLOWSHIP

I went to a Christian college that did not have an InterVarsity Christian Fellowship (IVCF) chapter, but many of my friends went to public and private secular institutions that did.

In every case, what sticks in my mind about their time with IVCF is both the regular discipleship and Bible studies they engaged in as well as their outreach and evangelism efforts among their classmates, campus and beyond. Their triennial Urbana Student Missions Conference has been running for decades and has helped thousands of students—including some from my local church—discern and follow God's call to the global mission field.

At the same time, their emphasis on evangelism has become almost seamlessly integrated with an emphasis on social concern. For instance, the Urbana 2012 conference featured a moving in-person testimony from Shortie Khumalo, an AIDS victim caregiver from Swaziland. Attendees were then invited to respond to her message by writing notes of encouragement to other caregivers and by going to the floor of the main hall to help pack AIDS Caregiver Kits. In just two hours they had boxed a total of 32,000 kits that World Vision later shipped to partners in African countries.

York Moore is the national evangelist for InterVarsity, and in this role he trains students in evangelism while also organizing "Justice Invitationals" across America. In 2010 York partnered with International Justice Mission, World Vision, and the Not for Sale Campaign to organize "The Price of Life," a campaign at Ohio State University to increase awareness of human trafficking.

They built seventeen interactive art displays known as "proxe stations" across the OSU campus to raise awareness about modern-day slavery and draw the connections between justice and Jesus. Over the course of five days they also held fourteen events, a nine-hundred-person-strong march along part of the Underground Railroad, and a town hall with state and federal officials. At the end of the campaign over three hundred students decided to follow Christ and over twenty thousand were exposed to the reality of the modern-day slave trade. One OSU student who stopped by a proxe station remarked that he sees a lot of people—especially in the news—who claim they're Christians but don't act like it. He went on to share that it was "really great to see an actual Christian group that's walking the walk."[14]

A MISSIONARY EXAMPLE: JACOB RODRIGUEZ

I lived with Jacob Rodriguez while he was in graduate school studying biblical exegesis and training to become a crosscultural missionary. My favorite part of being a housemate with Jake is that on most nights we would pray and sing hymns together before going to bed. Often overwhelmed with work, I looked forward to these worship times as an opportunity to recenter on God.

Even though he was not on his official "mission field" in Ethiopia yet, Jake viewed our surrounding low-income neighborhood as a mission field and poured himself into building relationships with the neighbors.

He loved our neighbors by simply sharing life with them. He would kick a soccer ball with the kids, join families for meals, come alongside those struggling with substance abuse problems, advocate on issues that affected our neighborhood such as immigration reform, and more. At the same time he also intentionally talked with our neighbors about his faith, found them Bibles in languages they could read and prayed both with and for them.

His rich ministry in our neighborhood was not an elaborate balancing act between evangelism and social concern. Rather, it flowed holistically from a burning passion Jake had for our neighbors to know Jesus and be rescued from the brokenness both in themselves and in the structures and society around them.

While writing this chapter, I emailed Jake, who is now training pastors at a Bible college in Ethiopia, to ask him how he sees evangelism and social justice connected in his current ministry. He was recovering from malaria at the time, but his response was typically thoughtful:

> Our verbal proclamation of the gospel must address issues of social justice, not by saying, "act justly to earn your salvation," but rather that "you have acted unjustly, so come to God for mercy and forgiveness, and he will transform you to act justly."
>
> In Ethiopia, preaching repentance from societal sin is utterly important. Most of my students come from very well-churched regions. But if there is a government official or businessman in their congregation, the preacher will not preach against corruption in the government or unjust business transactions. So people are coming to Christ and still giving bribes at work and not paying their workers just wages.

And when preachers preach repentance, there is very little mention of racial reconciliation. There are fifty-five people groups in southern Ethiopia, and there is frequently ethnic conflict and tribalism. How can we preach the gospel if we don't preach repentance? And how can we preach repentance if we don't preach racial reconciliation? There was a student in my school whose local church leader cut his scholarship because he was from a rival people group. Anemic gospel proclamations will only perpetuate this.

WHOLLY ON MISSION

Faithful social action means that we cannot truly seek justice without doing it in the name of Christ.

And seeking justice isn't just a door or a gateway through which we can bring in the gospel. It's an indispensable part of the gospel itself. It's also a natural outcome of Jesus' presence in our lives and in the world. To pursue social action as a scheme to soften people into being more open to evangelism is both disingenuous and misguided. As Tim Keller puts it, "A life poured out in doing justice for the poor is the inevitable sign of any real, true gospel faith."[15]

Looking back after a decade of activism, I now realize that the tension I used to feel between evangelism and social action was unnecessary. Just as Jesus held the two together throughout his holistic ministry, there has never been a time when I've had to choose between sharing and showing my faith. Instead, they've continued to come together within a holistic gospel and mission. The more I pursue God's kingdom through social action, the more I have reason and opportunity to tell others about God's salvation through Christ's death and resurrection.

Surely this is closer to what it means to be on mission with God.

FOR REFLECTION AND APPLICATION

1. On the one hand, there is an often-expressed view that a younger generation of Christians in America "is in the process of swinging

away from evangelism and toward the social gospel." On the other hand, there is the view that an older generation of Christians in America "focused so exclusively on evangelism that they largely neglected social justice. And when they did engage on social issues it was skewed toward fighting the culture wars and selectively (often hypocritically) targeting issues of personal and sexual immorality while ignoring if not perpetuating other social and economic injustices." How have these often-expressed statements of deeply held views affected you personally?

2. Spend some time looking at Colossians 1:15-23. How does this passage challenge the idea that God has given up on the world he made and that his agenda is simply to save human souls out of it?

3. The Lausanne Movement is recovering "the biblical truth that the gospel is God's good news, through the cross and resurrection of Jesus Christ, for individual persons, and for society, and for creation. All three are broken and suffering because of sin; all three are included in the redeeming love and mission of God; all three must be part of the comprehensive mission of God's people." As a person interested in social justice, how does this biblical truth help or challenge you?

4. Have you ever known someone who had that holistic understanding of the gospel, someone like Jacob Rodriguez, who wanted his "neighbors to know Jesus and be rescued from the brokenness both in themselves and in the structures and society around them"? Tell the group about this person.

5. From this holistic gospel perspective, pray through this passage: "Therefore go and make disciples of all nations, baptizing them in the name of the Father and of the Son and of the Holy Spirit, and teaching them to obey everything I have commanded you. And surely I am with you always, to the very end of the age" (Matthew 28:19-20).

5

TRANSCENDING THE CULTURE WARS

Do not be overcome by evil, but
overcome evil with good.

ROMANS 12:21

THE COLD RAIN PELTED DOWN in near horizontal sheets as I dashed from the car to the train station platform, campaign staff in tow.

This was by far the worst storm of autumn, but there were a lot of stations in the district that we still needed to get to before the election. The morning commute was a great opportunity to introduce myself to potential voters as they waited for their trains into the city. It may have been miserable outside, but no one seemed to mind as I jumped into the crowd and started shaking hands: "Hi, I'm Ben Lowe, and I'm running for Congress in this district!" A campaign volunteer followed behind me handing out campaign brochures and other voting information.

Things were going pretty well until a middle-aged woman stalked up with a scowl: "You women-hater," she growled as she stuffed the campaign flyer back into my hands, "I'd vote for a monkey before I'd ever vote for you!"

I knew immediately what she was upset about. Breaking from my Republican family heritage, I was running as a pro-life Democrat (more later on why), which did not sit well with the largely pro-choice Democratic base. Many of them saw me as just another man opposing the rights of women to have control over their own bodies.

As the angry commuter disappeared into the crowd I took a deep breath and forced myself to move on. Before long, the next train arrived and I stepped back to let folks board. This train marked the end of the morning commute, and I breathed a deep sigh of relief: it's draining for an introvert like me to put myself out there. As I turned to go, however, an older man in a suit brushed hurriedly past me to catch the train, pausing just long enough to mutter, "Get out of here, you Democrat! You're just another baby killer."

Lord. Have. Mercy. I thought. *I know the Democratic party platform is officially pro-choice, but does that automatically make me a "baby killer," even though I'm pro-life? And by running as a pro-life candidate, does that somehow make me a "women hater" too?*

Welcome to the Culture Wars

The culture wars have defined much of our Christian witness for the last generation and continue to be a major force in the church and culture today. For those in more homogeneous contexts where ideological differences don't bump up against each other much, this may seem relatively irrelevant and overblown. For others who are active on the frontlines of controversial or polarized issues, however, the warring may be only too real and pervasive.

A lot can be said to describe and analyze the culture wars, but at its heart is a power struggle between two loosely defined but passionate and well-intentioned ideological factions in American society: conservatives on the right versus progressives on the left, and, particularly, religious conservatives versus secular progressives.[1] In political terms this often but imperfectly translates into Republicans versus Democrats.

The warring has been fiercest around a range of social issues—abortion, sexuality and marriage, and religious freedom in particular. Gun control, stem cell research, creation versus evolution, and now healthcare reform, immigration reform and climate action are often also on the hit list. Sound polarizing enough yet?

A COMPLICATED HERITAGE

Although my family served as missionaries in Asia during much of my childhood, I still grew up heavily influenced by the Caucasian American evangelical subculture. We rarely discussed politics at home, though I knew that my father and his father, and his father's father, always voted Republican. To me, being pro-life, pro-family, and pro-Christian America was just part of being a good patriotic believer. I knew my place on the "right" side of the culture wars.

Moving to the United States and coming of age in a post-9/11 era, however, I began to realize that this worldview was flawed and incomplete. America really isn't a Christian nation (never mind what our money says—we certainly don't act Christlike) and our track record as a beacon of justice and freedom is mixed at best. This doesn't negate all the good that we've done in our country and around the world, but it doesn't ignore the great harm we've caused either.

I also realized that to care about what God cares about sometimes means siding with Republican positions, sometimes with Democratic positions and sometimes with neither. Neither party fully represented my values, and neither party had a monopoly on my support.

Even the evangelical community, which claimed to have God's solutions, seemed to be contributing an awful lot to the problems. I was deeply troubled by our pervasive cultural accommodation, the skewed political track record of the religious right (with its entanglement with the Republican Party), and our obsession with a few key social issues at the expense of many other biblical priorities.[2] And I was sick of the way our faith was being shamelessly manipulated and abused for political ends by both the right and left.

AN UNAVOIDABLE REALITY

The more I read the Bible, the more the culture wars seemed misguided, and the more I mourned the damage they were causing in the misleading name of "reclaiming America for Christ." Like many of my millennial peers, I want nothing to do with perpetuating the culture wars of the past.

For this and other reasons, I almost didn't include this chapter in the book. When I shared the first draft with some friends, I received such strong negative feedback about the topic that I contemplated cutting it out altogether. Does giving the culture wars so much attention not just further exacerbate the problem?

The reality, however, is that the culture wars are still our unavoidable backdrop and context for social action today. They're constantly in play as we—and our leaders and churches—weigh in on societal debates and exert our influence on policies, elections, ballot initiatives and so forth. Ignoring the culture wars won't make them go away, and, contrary to occasional predictions in the press, there's little indication that they're winding down any time soon.

So how can we learn from our history and *transcend* the culture wars in constructive and redemptive ways?

BREAKING DOWN STEREOTYPES

One obvious challenge to discussing all of this is that the culture wars are a lot more nuanced than I have or can easily describe.

To start with, not all people of faith are conservative, and not all agnostics or atheists are liberal. There are many religious progressives as well as secular conservatives, and there are many moderates and others who don't fit comfortably with any of these labels. By today's standards a lot of us could be characterized as being politically or socially conservative in some ways but progressive in others.

More specifically, not all evangelical Christians are Republicans. While this attribution might be somewhat fair for the vast majority of *Caucasian* evangelicals who consistently vote for the Republican presidential candidate (79 percent voted for Mitt Romney in 2012, for instance),[3] what about the significant populations of Latino, African American and other evangelicals who don't? Not only do these groups tend to vote overwhelmingly Democratic—often for good scriptural reasons related to social and economic justice—but they also don't seem quite so exclusively focused on the narrow slate of traditional culture wars issues such as abortion and gay marriage.

So whatever we say about the culture wars, it's important to note that it does not represent all of us. There is great diversity in the body of Christ, and we can recognize and celebrate this better.

CULTURE WARS CASUALTIES

The problem with the culture wars is not just *what* is being fought over but *how* it's being fought, as Christian social critic Os Guinness notes:

> Name-calling, insult, ridicule, guilt by association, caricature, in-nuendo, accusation, denunciation, negative ads, and deceptive and manipulative videos have replaced deliberation and debate. Neither side talks to the other side, only about them; and there is no pretense of democratic engagement, let alone a serious effort at persuasion. Needless to say, the culture-war industry is lucrative as well as politically profitable, and a swelling band of profiteering culture warriors are rushing to strike gold with their wild attacks on the other side, all for the consumption of their own supporters and the promotion of their books and programs. But the toll of such trench warfare on the republic is heavy.[4]

Guinness is blunt but fair in his criticism. Beyond the truncated agendas and unholy political alliances, too many Christians have been fighting the culture wars in an overwhelmingly combative and divisive way, focused on building walls instead of bridges. It has become much more about demonizing the other side in order to further galvanize the base rather than respectfully trying to negotiate areas of agreement and progress.

As Eric Hoffer once noted, "Mass movements can rise and spread without belief in a God, but never without belief in a devil."[5] Strategists on both sides of the culture wars have found this to be true: the more alarming the threat, the more inflammatory the rhetoric and the more confrontational the stance, the bigger the response from their base of loyalists.

And the media, which has largely capitulated to our demand for entertainment over information, is only elevating the vitriol and intensifying the polarization. Meanwhile, those who try to reach out with a more moderate and conciliatory approach are often threatened and bullied.

Though others may fight like this, aren't Christians supposed to be different?

This adversarial approach has left a lot of people, both inside and outside of the faith, increasingly disillusioned and disaffected by Christianity and its role in the public square. Leaders such as sociologist Robert Putnam argue that disillusionment with the overly political religious right is one of the major reasons the millennial generation is leaving the church in droves.[6]

Jesus said that the world would know us by our love. But when David Kinnaman and Gabe Lyons conducted an in-depth survey of what young Americans thought of Christianity, the overwhelming response was that Christians are judgmental, anti-homosexual, hypocritical, too political and sheltered.[7]

This is deeply troubling. We want people to know Jesus, but our shrill, narrow and often hyperpartisan public witness is driving them away. Gratefully, some of this seems to be changing.

RUMBLINGS OF CHANGE

As new generations of Christians rise to take on more leadership, and as the old guard of the religious right fades away, there is growing enthusiasm to reclaim our faith and renew our engagement in the world. The most visible sign that things are changing is the growing push to take more biblically holistic stands on current issues, coupled with a less partisan approach to politics.

New faith-based movements have risen up, along with numerous causes and declarations, such as the Evangelical Immigration Table and the Evangelical Climate Initiative. Acting on AIDS, a student initiative sponsored by World Vision, impacted campuses around the nation for many years. Invisible Children and other anti-human-trafficking initiatives have spread like wildfire across both church and society. Racial reconciliation remains an ongoing concern, and both community development and poverty alleviation have become priority issues as well.

In a sense these have been heady and hope-filled times. Many of us, especially in the millennial generation, have been enthusiastically engaged in this fresh wave of social action. The media has jumped into the fray as well, ratcheting up the excitement and expectations with story after story proclaiming that a great sea change is under way in American Christianity; a "new evangelicalism" is rising and is transforming both the church and the world.

In another sense, however, much still hasn't changed. In many evangelical circles there has been stubborn opposition to much of this progress. And while the religious right is becoming increasingly marginalized in both church and society, the culture wars themselves remain very much alive.

MOVING FORWARD

Many of us from conservative backgrounds want the culture to be what it was like when we were growing up. It was safe and comfortable for us then—but it wasn't for many others, as Ed Stetzer, a Southern Baptist leader and the president of LifeWay Research, wrote in *Christianity Today* when the Supreme Court struck down the Defense of Marriage Act in 2013:

> Fifty years ago, Christians comprised the mainstream in America and were fully accepted as a cultural majority. Many during that

time did not stand up for those who were weak and marginalized. The "good old days" so often longed for were also times of racial oppression, gender discrimination, and theological confusion. So, pining for those "moral" days of yore is like chasing a mirage. The past simply wasn't that great for many when Christians had more influence.[8]

The cultural landscape continues to evolve today, presenting both challenges and opportunities. How will Christians respond? Will we pull back and silo ourselves from the public square again? Will we retrench in the culture wars of the past? Or will we learn from our mistakes and find a more faithful way forward?

With the goal of responding constructively, here are six steps toward transcending the culture wars, renewing our public witness and finding common ground for the common good.

1. Pursue a holistic vision over a narrow vision. One day, early on in his ministry, Jesus read from the scroll of Isaiah to a crowd eager to hear what he had to expound to them from the Scriptures. He began,

The Spirit of the Lord is on me,
  because he has anointed me
  to proclaim good news to the poor.
He has sent me to proclaim freedom for the prisoners
  and recovery of sight for the blind,
to set the oppressed free,
  to proclaim the year of the Lord's favor. (Luke 4:18-19)

When he finished reading, he sat down and told the people that they were witnessing the fulfillment of this age-old prophecy within their midst. The Nazareth Declaration had been proclaimed. This was Jesus' manifesto on his mission and the scope of his concern. And it is broader than the triumvirate of abortion, gay marriage and religious freedom. His concern reaches to the poor, the captives, the blind and the oppressed. As a tour of the rest of Luke confirms, Jesus' mandate extends beyond preaching eternal salvation to also addressing physical, social and economic needs. It's a vision of the Messiah ushering in the kingdom of God on earth through a holistic mission that includes salvation for the whole person, healing from brokenness and freedom from injustice.

In Christ we find an agenda that is broad and balanced, and the outpouring of a pure heart of love. As the body of Christ, therefore, there is no biblical basis for limiting our agenda to a few select issues (more on this in chap. 6).

2. Renew our means, not just our ends. Out of zeal to win the culture wars and amass social and political power, many Christians have supported shameful tactics and have compromised their integrity. They have fallen prey to the corrupting lie that the right ends can justify the wrong means. But, as Martin Luther King Jr. insisted, "the means we use must be as pure as the ends we seek. . . . It is wrong to use immoral means to attain moral ends."[9] Both our ends and our means need to faithfully reflect the Jesus we represent.

What do faithful tactics look like and how is Christ-centered activism distinct from other approaches to organizing and social change? One helpful resource on this topic is *Faith-Rooted Organizing*, coauthored by Alexia Salvatierra and Peter Heltzel.[10]

But to start with, we can champion civility and integrity in the public square. We can talk with each other and not just at or about each other. We can do the hard but invaluable work of building trust with all people and learning to love even our enemies. We can honestly represent the positions of those who differ from us, and we can be open to collaboration with them. And we can be ready to consider solutions based on their merit and not the ideological label they carry. For some, this will involve the challenging process of untangling their worldview so that their faith defines their political ideology and not the other way around.

3. Accept that America is not a Christian nation. Good books have been written to deconstruct the false notion that America was

founded as a Christian nation and that we should return to our supposed biblical founding principles.[11] America was founded on a
general belief in a higher power and a firm commitment to religious
freedom for all. And our national operating manual is the US Consti-
tution, not the Bible. As such, the separation of church and state is a
good thing when done right, and there are distinctions between the
standards of holiness that we cultivate among Christians and the expectations we share with the rest of society.

Furthermore, the global church, not any particular nation-state, is
God's chosen people today. Tim Keller puts it this way, "Christians
now do not constitute a theocratic kingdom-state, but exist as an international communion of local assemblies living in every nation and
culture, under many different governments to whom they give great
respect but never absolute allegiance."[12]

4. Emphasize our public witness beyond our political witness.
Not everything in life is about political power. Politics is important,
but our public witness is much larger than that. This is where the
religious right has done a lot of good that often goes unnoticed: they
care for the incarcerated, the poor, the homeless, the orphan and more.
Their collective practical works of mercy are unrivaled in the recent
history of Christianity in America and are worth commending and
continuing with respect and appreciation.

Take Focus on the Family, the megaministry founded by the often
controversial Dr. James Dobson. Only about 5 percent of their budget
has actually ever gone to their public policy programs. The rest is
poured into counseling, communication tools, emergency aid and
other family resources. Over the past thirty years Focus on the Family
has helped save countless marriages and families from falling apart.
They've mobilized around adoption and have given immeasurable resources and time to the poor and sick. They've even paid electric bills
and mortgages for people in financial need. It's a shame that much of
the private ministry aspect goes unnoticed and the more controversial
public witness aspect ends up defining our faith the most.

5. Find a third way. One of the best ways we can transcend the culture wars is by moving beyond the two opposing ideological poles to pursue a third and higher road.

Jesus is our perfect model. The Jewish religious leaders repeatedly tried to trap him with their questions, but he astutely avoided their schemes and found a third way forward. "Let any one of you who is without sin be the first person to throw a stone at her," he said of the woman caught in adultery (John 8:7), and, "give back to Caesar what is Caesar's, and to God what is God's," he replied when asked if it was right to pay the imperial tax (Matthew 22:21; Mark 12:17; Luke 20:25).

Over the summer of 2012, Dan Cathy, the president of the popular fast-food chain Chick-fil-A, made public comments opposing homosexuality and gay marriage. Intense media coverage ensued and caused a cultural firestorm.[13] LGBT activists began calling for a Chick-fil-A boycott, which led conservatives to respond with Chick-fil-A Day, where thousands of Christians descended on their local stores and consumed copious amounts of fried and grilled chicken.

Around this time, Dan began reaching out to Shane Windmeyer, the leader of Campus Pride, an LGBT organization that was actively protesting Chick-fil-A. Over time they developed a relationship of mutual respect and trust as they stepped back from the caustic culture warring to understand each other as "people with opposing views, not as opposing people."[14]

Neither Dan nor Shane has changed what they ultimately believe about sexuality or marriage. But this vulnerable and intentional friendship eventually led to Chick-fil-A strengthening its policies, practices and charitable giving to more faithfully "treat every person with honor, dignity, and respect." In turn, Campus Pride ended its protest campaign against the restaurant chain. Shane also penned a moving article about this unexpected friendship that went viral on *Huffington Post*. He writes, "Gay and straight, liberal and conservative, activist and evangelist—we could stand together in our difference and in our respect. How much better would our world be if more could do the same?"[15]

According to the culture wars, Dan and Shane were enemies who had every reason to hate and oppose each other. Instead, they were able to find a better way forward by transcending the warfare to grow together as friends.

6. Move forward with humility. Young activists like myself sometimes (foolishly and arrogantly) think that our generation will finally get it all right. We won't. Every generation has its own truncated view of reality, and mine is certainly no exception. We will continue to make mistakes in the future, no matter how well-intentioned we are.

The quest for faithfulness in our social action requires the wisdom and strength that God makes available through the Holy Spirit and the "cloud of witnesses" who have gone before. We can all learn from the past. We are not better than they, but because of their successes and sacrifices we can see things that others couldn't.

A Story of Hope

It's impossible for me to think about the culture wars without also thinking of my good friend Amy Tracy.

I got to know Amy soon after my congressional campaign ended. (I lost the election with 37 percent of the vote.) She sent me a Facebook message from Colorado Springs thanking me for running and mentioning, to my surprise, that she had worked for Focus on the Family. As we messaged back and forth, Amy shared more of her remarkable story, which has also been written up in a couple *Christianity Today* articles.[16]

Earlier in her life Amy was the youngest-ever press secretary for the influential National Organization of Women (NOW). As an outspoken lesbian activist, Amy was on the front lines of the culture wars, physically putting herself in harm's way during violent Christian protests in front of abortion clinics.

Through it all God somehow got ahold of Amy, though it wasn't through the vicious and spiteful Christians she encountered during some of the protests. Eventually she gave her life to following Jesus.

She also left NOW and, in an ironic twist, went to work for Focus on the Family as an aide to their president and culture warrior Dr. James Dobson.

Being on the other side of the culture wars was a painful experience for Amy: "I definitely felt more beat up and more disillusioned on the right . . . mostly because so much of what was said and how it was said ran contrary to Scripture. It crushed my faith and it's been a long journey to get back with Jesus Christ."[17] Amy eventually left Focus. She is now happily serving in an international missions and publishing agency during the day and a hospice ministry at night.

Healing from her bad experiences of working first for the left and then for the right has been a slow, hard and ongoing process. Through this journey, however, Amy has somehow found a way to respect and remain friends with both her former NOW colleagues and her former Focus colleagues. Although she experienced firsthand the vitriol of the culture wars on both sides, she has found a way to push through to a life of love and redemption.

Amy is not an activist for the left or for the right anymore. Today, she's first and foremost a servant and follower of Christ, which is as it should be for all of us.

Stories like Amy's give me great hope. They remind me that, in the ugly mess of the culture wars, change is still possible, and God is still very much at work reconciling all things and all people—even the staunchest liberals and die-hard conservatives—back to himself through Jesus' blood shed on the cross (Colossians 1:15-20).

FOR REFLECTION AND APPLICATION

1. Are you personally aware of people who have left the church because of the culture wars, or who are antagonistic to Jesus because of the culture wars? If so, please tell their stories to the group.

2. For you personally, how have you dealt with the reality of the culture wars? By fighting in it? By ignoring it? By speaking out

against it? By reaching out to those waging it or those victimized by it? Explain.

3. Take a long and careful look at John 8:1-11. How was Jesus caught in the middle of that period's culture wars? Pay attention to the righteous zeal of the culture warriors, to Jesus' long silence, to their repeated questioning. How did Jesus respond and not respond? Which side, if any, did he take? Who did he defend? Is there something about how Jesus handled this that can be an example for us today in navigating our culture wars?

4. If Jesus represents the third way in the opposing sides of the culture wars, do you personally know anyone who is following his example? In what specific ways does that person's life represent Jesus' third way?

5. Given Jesus' example of dealing with the culture wars, and given the good examples of modern-day Christ followers, pray for the Holy Spirit's help to live out this verse: "Do not be overcome by evil, but overcome evil with good" (Romans 12:21).

6

RESTORING A FAITHFUL AGENDA

*If you really change your ways and your actions
and deal with each other justly, if you do not oppress the foreigner,
the fatherless or the widow and do not shed innocent blood in this
place, and if you do not follow other gods to your own harm,
then I will let you live in this place, in the land
I gave your ancestors for ever and ever.*

JEREMIAH 7:5-7

THE REVEREND MITCH HESCOX WAITED, calm and unbowed, as the congressman from Illinois continued his angry tirade from behind the bench at the front of the hearing room.

The congressman fired question after question at the Reverend, barely pausing to take a breath. At one point Mitch leaned into his microphone and asked if he could respond, to which the congressman shot back, "I think I'm doing pretty well on my own here."

He wasn't looking for actual answers. He seemed far more interested in using his position on the committee as a bully pulpit to lash out at the pastor and—though he may not have realized—fellow Republican.

The Reverend Hescox began his career working in the coal industry and then went on to be a Methodist pastor in Pennsylvania for many years before taking on the role of president and CEO at the Evangelical Environmental Network (EEN).

On this particular day, he was giving testimony before the House Subcommittee on Energy and Power, in support of the new Mercury and Air Toxics Standards (MATS) that the EPA was enacting through the Clean Air Act. The long-awaited pollution standards, which took a full twenty years to research and develop, are designed to cut back on the amount of dangerous toxins—such as mercury—that coal-fired power plants are allowed to emit, thus protecting the lives and health of many people.

In America, mercury poisoning affects developing babies more than any other segment of our population. Babies accumulate mercury through their mothers, who ingest it by eating tainted fish and other foods. The fish get mercury when the neurotoxin settles out of air pollution and bioaccumulates up the aquatic food chain. Our mother's womb is designed to be one of the safest and most nurturing places in the world, but today one in six American babies is born with unsafe levels of mercury in their systems.[1]

The congressman from Illinois was irate because EEN was running an advocacy campaign—complete with radio, TV and billboard ads in key congressional districts—championing the mercury rule as an example of pro-life legislation. The congressman claims to be pro-life, but he is also heavily funded by the fossil fuel industry, which is the largest emitter of domestic mercury pollution in the United States today.[2] So he accused EEN's campaign of trying to hijack what it means to be pro-life. According to him, "The 'life' in 'pro-life' denotes not the quality of life, but life itself."[3]

But a holistic and consistent pro-life ethic isn't just about opposing abortion—it's also about protecting life in all stages, from conception to natural death. So it's ironic that many pro-life legislators regularly oppose environmental regulations, when one of the best ways to protect life at all stages is to protect the air, water, food and other natural resources that we depend on in order to flourish. When the land isn't healthy, people aren't healthy.

The coal lobby is powerful, however, and they wield their clout persuasively. As a result, some influential congressional leaders came out in opposition to the MATS rule. They launched an all-out effort to overrule the EPA's efforts, employing a rarely used tool that allows members of Congress to bring executive actions like the pollution rule up for a vote. The vote was close. Too close. But in the end the rule survived and has since begun to be implemented. The result is that some of the most outdated and dirtiest coal-fired power plants in the nation have had to either update their pollution control technology or begin shutting down.

Shortly after the MATS rule survived the congressional challenge, EEN received messages of thanks from the EPA and other groups, including the American Lung Association, where a senior official told Mitch Hescox, "You folks at EEN can sleep easy tonight, for you just helped save the lives of millions of children."[4] It turns out that were it not for some of the pro-life legislators that EEN helped bring on board through their advocacy efforts, the rule would likely not have survived.

No one expected Christians—and evangelicals at that—to be among the key players in achieving stricter mercury pollution standards across the United States. Given the last fifty years of culture warring, EEN's efforts frankly caught people by surprise. Hopefully this reputation is changing, however, as we increasingly turn back to the Bible for a richer and fuller understanding of what God is calling us to care about.

RENEWING OUR AGENDA

For decades some Christian leaders—such as Ron Sider, Jim Wallis and Tony Campolo—have championed a whole-life ethic that values and protects human life from conception to natural death or "from womb to tomb." Such an ethic includes care for the environment, just economic policies, strong education systems, the protection of human rights, the promotion of peace over war, the abolition of nuclear weapons and much more.

But these leaders have often struggled to gain traction with the bulk of politically conservative Christians. Instead, due to the culture wars, tension between evangelism and social action and other factors, our social agenda and therefore our public witness has been checkered with shortcomings and blind spots.

Moving forward, what does it look like to renew our agenda so that it is more faithful to the Scriptures? I propose three principles, beginning first with our focus, and then progressing deeper to consider our approach and our motivation.

1. Our focus: From narrow to holistic. As I touched on in chapter five, our stereotypical—or perhaps, typical—social agenda is too narrow, arbitrary and exclusive.

As it stands, many leaders of the now-fading religious right truncated their involvement in the public square to the triumvirate of opposing abortion, opposing gay marriage and fighting for religious freedom for Christians.

These three issues supposedly have to be *the* priority for all Christians. Proponents concede that we may be called to address other concerns as well, but those are engaged on a case-by-case and person-by-person basis. They aren't first-order priorities for the whole church. And when others try to bring up broader issues, such as the Evangelical Environmental Network did with the mercury rule, some leaders associated with the religious right have dismissed these as divisive and distracting from our proper mission in America.

As followers of Jesus Christ, our vision needs to be as big as God's vision and our mission as big as God's mission. The same Bible and the same Savior that call us to care for the unborn also calls us to care for the poor, the unemployed, the uninsured, the sick, the handicapped, the malnourished, the environment, refugees, child soldiers, prisoners, slaves, orphans, widows and so on.

If the Bible doesn't prioritize among these issues, why should we? While each of us seeks to discern and follow our individual calling, the body of Christ is called to take a bigger and more holistic view. Yes, Christians should care about abortion, marriage and religious freedom. But shouldn't we also care about health care reform, unemployment benefits, credit card abuses, fair wages, education reform, clean energy, nuclear proliferation, racial reconciliation and all the other social concerns in the world today?

Such a broader concern is growing among Christians of all political leanings. Particularly since the turn of this century, Christians have been engaging in an increasingly diverse range of causes, and often to good effect. The highly successful pro-life campaign that EEN led in support of the Mercury and Air Toxics Standards is just one example out of many. EEN itself has gone from being a more marginalized group in the church to being an active member of the highly respected National Association of Evangelicals.

As another example, it wasn't so long ago that much of the church viewed HIV/AIDS purely as a stigma of immoral lifestyles and a punishment from God. Today, however, we've played a significant and ongoing role in stemming the tide of HIV/AIDS in the world and caring for the many orphans and communities that have been hit the hardest by this scourge. President George W. Bush, an evangelical who was closely advised on this issue by other Christians, created the massive and groundbreaking Presidents Emergency Plan for AIDS Relief (PEPFAR). PEPFAR has helped save the lives of millions of AIDS victims around the world and has proved to be a hallmark achievement of compassionate conservatism and one of the greatest foreign aid success stories of all time.

2. Our approach: From against to for. Second, we need to renew our underlying approach to social action. Christians are often and unnecessarily known more for what we are against than for what we are for.

Traditionally, this has been true both on a personal level (don't drink, don't smoke, don't do drugs, don't get tattoos, don't watch graphic movies, don't date non-Christians, don't have sex outside marriage) and on a societal level (we're against same-sex marriage, against liberals, against abortion, against secularization, against fun). Okay, maybe not the last one, but you get the point.

Our approach to how we live and how we view the rest of the world often appears to boil down to a long list of what we oppose rather than what we champion. It starts sounding more like the endless traditions the Pharisees were burdening people with—without so much as lifting a finger to help them—rather than the timeless gospel Jesus came to proclaim (Luke 11:46). It's no wonder we're often known as being judgmental and, inevitably, hypocritical.

Christians are called to be a holy people, set apart for the purposes and worship of God. We're called to be in but not of the world, so in some important ways we will always be distinct from those around us. Blending in is not the goal. But we've taken the art of sticking out to a new (and bad) level. Some of this is a matter of communication, or what some call branding or marketing, but at other times it runs deeper to our actual intentions.

By opposing premarital sex, for instance, the biblical intention is not to be overly restrictive or prudish, but to value and honor the gift of sex as God created it to be cherished—within the covenantal bonds of marriage. Furthermore, sex within a healthy marriage helps to ensure that it remains a mutually beneficial act of love versus a selfish and often harmful act of lust. However, it takes work to understand, articulate and communicate these values. Sometimes we're just lazy— and sometimes the media and outside observers are lazy too—and would rather fall back on a clear, and sometimes arbitrary, list of rules and regulations. After all, it's far easier to list what we are against than to explain what we are for and why.

Consider once again what it means to be pro-life. While *pro-life* is very positive and winsome branding, in reality it's too often just about opposing abortion. This explains why some pro-life legislators were so offended by Mitch Hescox's testimony and EEN's campaign connecting mercury pollution with being pro-life. By extending our concern beyond only abortion, however, we can be comprehensively and consistently *for* human life in all its sacred stages.

Furthermore, being truly pro-life when it does come to the issue of abortion means caring for both the life of the baby *and the mother*. After all, the mother's life counts too, and the reality is that being pro-life often ends up more accurately described as being pro-baby but anti-mother.

Few issues are more painful, private and polarizing than the issue of abortion. I cannot imagine the stark realities and life-altering decisions that women face when they find themselves in an unplanned, unwanted or unsafe pregnancy.

At the same time, however, life begins at conception and is sacred. As Wendell Berry proposes, two central questions to ask about abortion are "Is it killing? And what is killed?"[5] The reality, as Berry goes on to affirm, is that

> To kill is the express purpose of the procedure. What is killed is usually described by apologists for abortion as "a fetus," as if that term names a distinct kind of species of being. But what this being might be, if it is not a human being, is not clear. Generally pregnant women have thought and spoken of the beings in their wombs as "babies." The attempt to make a categorical distinction between a baby living in the womb and a baby living in the world is as tenuous as would be an attempt to make such a distinction between a living child and a living adult. No living creature is "viable" independently of an enveloping life-support system.[6]

Those who favor abortion rights often and appropriately cite tragic instances of rape, incest or risks to the life of the mother, and describe their position as giving women the right to choose what happens to their bodies. In this sense abortion is a human rights conflict. On one hand the mother may claim the right to particular closely guarded liberties; on the other, the baby has the right to life. When an abortion is considered, there are rarely ever winners on either side, only casualties, victims and survivors.

What if instead of simply choosing between supporting the baby or the mother, we make every effort to be both pro-baby and pro-mother? What if we did everything possible to reduce the demand for abortions and come alongside women in crisis? While it still won't make everyone happy—that's not the goal anyway—both pro-life and pro-choice advocates can agree on numerous things here.

We do well to learn from former congressman and ambassador Tony Hall of Ohio. When Hall came to faith after taking office, he changed from being pro-choice to pro-life. He didn't, however, simply check off the "pro-life" box on candidate surveys and then stay on the sidelines. Rather, he devoted significant energy and resources to working together with both sides of the issue and across the aisle on legislation that would help ensure that fewer women would ever resort to abortion for financial or social reasons.

Instead of ostracizing single or unwed mothers, Christians can come alongside them to provide the spiritual, emotional and financial support to help them keep their children. The Vineyard Church of Ann Arbor, Michigan, under the leadership of the late Pastor Nancy Wilson and her husband Senior Pastor Ken Wilson, is one of a growing number of churches leading the way in developing programs and fellowship groups for single parents. Likewise, many Christians have also been advocating for their churches to become more active on the adoption front so that over time there will be fewer and fewer orphans or unwanted babies.

I could go on to consider any number of other issues, but hopefully you get the picture. Instead of simply opposing particular positions on a short list of issues, Christians can champion a creative and constructive social agenda that is defined primarily by what we affirm and the solutions we initiate to the problems of the day. Christians should be known more by what we are for than what we are against.

3. *Our motivation: From fear to courage.* Finally, we need to renew our social agenda from being largely driven by fear to being driven by courage, which comes from love. For when we are controlled by fear we lose our ability to love.

One of the reasons many pro-life members of Congress opposed the EPA regulations mentioned earlier in this chapter is because they were being lobbied aggressively by some of the energy utilities. These corporations were afraid that cleaning up their pollution to comply with the rule would increase the cost of producing electricity. They would then have to either absorb these previously externalized costs or else pass them on to consumers in the unpopular form of higher energy bills. Not wanting to do either, they pressured legislators—who in this era of unlimited special interest political spending are ever fearful of offending their corporate donors—to obstruct the long-anticipated regulations.

In this case the energy corporations could have exhibited the courage to do the right thing and start cleaning up the toxins they produce as byproducts of burning coal, which are harming the health of millions of innocent people. And some of them are doing this. But others acted out of fear and greed, since they were going to lose some of their profits, and so they tried to stymie responsible action.

The legislators who opposed the regulations could have shown the courage to see beyond the influence of special interests and partisanship to consider the common good and the real human health costs of producing cheap but dirty energy. Instead of letting the EPA do its work, however, they chose to interfere out of fear, based in the self-interest of their political and reelection prospects.

As these energy utilities and elected officials illustrate, money and power—and the fear of losing money or power—can exert a corrupting and often overwhelming influence over many.

The Evangelical Environmental Network and their campaign partners were not numb to fear—it's intimidating and potentially costly to go up against powerful special interests and angry members of Congress. But spurred on by the biblical command to love their neighbors, they held to the courage of their convictions and stood up for what was right, in spite of having modest resources and facing stiff opposition. This is what it can look like to move from an agenda motivated by fear to one motivated by courage and based in love.

Our society subsists on a steady diet of fear: fear of terrorists, Muslims, socialists, immigrants, homosexuals, the poor and the list goes on. Much of this is based on our lust for comfort, control and security. Anything or anyone, known but especially unknown, that may threaten our lifestyle is viewed with fear and treated with hostility.

Shame on those who stoke our fears to prey and profit off of us! Politicians, media outlets, talk shows, discussion boards, radio shows and even certain church leaders have played a part in heightening our angst and ratcheting up our anxiety levels.

As the Christian social critic Os Guinness reminded me when I was running for Congress, the most commonly repeated commandment in the Bible is "do not fear." Tyler Wigg-Stevenson agrees: "Fear is the favorite weapon of every earthly principality, which is precisely why the Bible's consistent witness to the alternative, the kingdom of God, is so punctuated with injunctions for the faithful to 'fear not.'"[7]

We're called to order our lives around God's kingdom, not obsess over the anxieties and uncertainties of the world (Matthew 6). The God of the universe is more than able to equip and defend us as we pursue his calling. Faithful social action involves overcoming—not manipulating—our fears and prejudices to engage the actual facts with biblical faith, hope and love. After all, courage is not the absence of fear but the commitment to do the right thing in spite of being afraid. That's what should define our social agenda.

Moving Forward

With these three principles in mind, what should our social agenda specifically look like today? In other words, what is the right Christian position on the many justice issues we face? This is an important question, but one that intentionally lies beyond the scope of this book.

First, wiser and more experienced leaders have already published entire books focused on what they believe a Christian perspective on key social issues should look like. One good place to start is *For the Health of the Nation*, an official booklet put out by the National Association of Evangelicals that covers a number of key topics.[8]

Second, there are many legitimate differences among Christians when it comes to the details of sorting out the problems we're facing and proposing concrete solutions. As I asserted in chapter three, it's one thing to agree that we're called to love our neighbor, help the poor or care for creation. But what these shared values look like on the ground in specific instances can vary greatly and are open to rigorous and healthy debate. Sometimes there is a clear right versus wrong position or better versus worse approach. Often, however, there is no one obvious solution to the complicated problems we face. And it's usually presumptuous to claim that our position is *the* Christian position on an issue instead of *a* Christian position.

Developing an informed and biblically grounded social agenda is a task for each of us to pursue prayerfully, both on our own and in community. We'll make mistakes along the way, but that's not a reason to be paralyzed into inaction. Rather, we're called to take thoughtful stances and make responsible decisions based on the best knowledge we have available at the time. That's what it means to be a good steward.

We won't always be right, but over time, as we grow and learn, we'll have the opportunity to improve our positions so that we are always pursuing a more faithful agenda. One that is broad rather than narrow, positive rather than negative and courageous rather than fearful.

FOR REFLECTION AND APPLICATION

1. Some Christians have demanded that the American church focus exclusively on the three issues of opposing abortion, opposing gay marriage and supporting religious freedom for Christians. How

has this affected you personally and also affected the participation of other Christians in your particular area of social action?

2. Does your church encourage or practice the exclusive focus on these three issues? If so, how? Do you see change taking place in your church? Or does your church not have such a narrow focus? If so, why do you think it has escaped that narrow focus?

3. Regarding the stereotype that Christians are simply opposed to things, how do you—in your area of social action—escape that stereotype? What are you *for*, and how do you communicate that to people?

4. Despite the fact that we live in one of the safest, most secure and most prosperous countries in history, our society is dominated by fear. How, in your area of social action, can we move away from fear to becoming driven by faith, hope and love?

5. Pray for this to be true of us today:

> The Spirit of the Lord is on me,
>> because he has anointed me
>> to proclaim good news to the poor.
> He has sent me to proclaim freedom for the prisoners
>> and recovery of sight for the blind,
> to set the oppressed free,
>> to proclaim the year of the Lord's favor. (Luke 4:18-19)

PART TWO

SUSTAINING OUR ACTION

7

LOVE

This is how we know what love is:
Jesus Christ laid down his life for us.
And we ought to lay down our lives
for our brothers and sisters.

1 JOHN 3:16

If I am exceptionally eloquent and can impress people with my presence and personality, but do not have love, I am merely a windbag or a talking head.

If I'm brilliant and have great insight into complex problems, and if I am highly effective and productive, but do not have love, I'm not worth anything.

If I'm exceedingly generous with my resources, and personally sacrifice even to the point of suffering and death, but do not have love, I gain nothing.[1]

Sound familiar? It's not quite the same context or wording that the apostle Paul used when challenging the church in Corinth to remember the supremacy of love while desiring spiritual gifts (1 Corinthians 13), but his point carries over to how we approach social action as well: *no matter what we say, no matter what we know, and no matter what we do, none of it matters apart from love.*

Love, Not Hate

I spoke at a lot of gatherings during my congressional run, but one stands out in particular. It was a regular meeting of political activists, most of whom were supportive of my candidacy. Ahead of me on the program was a local union leader. His comments were less of a speech, however, and more of a rant. He railed against politicians who didn't support unions, warning us that they were not to be trusted. They're only out to hurt us and take food away from our children, he claimed, along with a whole assortment of other dramatic accusations geared toward alarming his audience into political action.

By the time it was my turn to speak, I was deeply troubled. It's one thing to argue that the policies of a particular party or politician are misguided and will have negative consequences. And it's true that some people really aren't trustworthy and should not be in public service. But it's a whole other matter to demonize everyone who disagrees with you by claiming that they are maliciously out to harm us and starve our families. Breeding fear and hate in order to stir people to action may seem effective, at least in the short term, but it's also wrong and dangerous. Animosity may be an easy wave to ride, but it ends only in destruction.

Standing in front of the group of fired-up political activists, I made the impromptu decision to shelve my regular stump speech and talk instead about love. About how hate destroys but love builds up. About how love should be our guide and motivation. And about how love can make us better people and a stronger community. I know this is not usually what people expect to hear from political candidates these days—after I got down someone commented that it sounded a bit like hippie talk—but perhaps it should be.

Too much of our social action, especially when it has to do with politics, often ends up being driven by the dark passions of hostility, bitterness, revenge and resentment. This is not who we are called to be, it's not what the world needs, and it will never bring healing and peace. In the words of Martin Luther King Jr., "Darkness cannot drive out darkness: only light can do that. Hate cannot drive out hate: only love can do that."[2]

As Christ followers we're called to engage in social action. And faithful social action is motivated through and through by love—love for God and love for our neighbor. In the first half of this book I addressed how we can renew our calling to social action. In this second half, I'm focusing on specific principles and practices that I've found critical to persevering faithfully in this calling. So I begin with love, because it lies at the very heart of who we are called to be and what we are called to do.

Love is why we care about justice in the first place. It's why we persevere even when things get hard, it's what keeps us patient when change comes slowly and it's what keeps us centered on Jesus throughout the struggle. Love guides our prophetic witness and emboldens us to exchange fear for courage. It leads us to repentance, subverts our selfish ambition and other idols, and gives us the strength to overcome opposition with grace. Love holds us when we rest from our striving, frees us up to partake in the sabbath, builds beloved community and invites us to turn our gaze to Jesus in worship.

Love is both the greatest gift and the greatest commandment, and all the good we try to do is only as good as the love we put into it. As Brother Lawrence put it, "We ought not to grow weary of doing little things for the love of God, who regards not the greatness of the work, but the love with which it is performed."[3]

GOD IS LOVE

Love is not our god, but our God is love, and his love is perfectly displayed through Jesus,

> Who, being in very nature God,
>   did not consider equality with God something to be used to
>   his own advantage;
> rather, he made himself nothing
>   by taking the very nature of a servant,
>   being made in human likeness.
> And being found in appearance as a man,
>   he humbled himself
>   by becoming obedient to death—
>   even death on a cross. (Philippians 2:6-8)

Jesus' incarnation, death and resurrection is the ultimate expression of God's love for us and for all the world.

During his earthly ministry Jesus further illustrated the scope of God's love through numerous parables and teachings. The parable of the prodigal son shows that God's love is all-encompassing, as the father joyfully welcomes home his wayward son and pleads with the indignant, self-righteous older brother to return as well. The parables of the lost sheep and the lost coin reveal that God is truly seeking and recovering the lost, and that each of us matters dearly to him.

In the Sermon on the Mount Jesus tells us to love our enemies because in doing so we become like our heavenly Father, who causes the sun to rise on the evil and good, and who makes rain to fall on both the righteous and unrighteous (Matthew 5:43-45). We are told to love our enemies because God loves his enemies, which at some point has included all of us (Romans 5:10).

In 1 Corinthians 13 the apostle Paul teaches that love is unfailing; it is patient and kind; it's not envious, boastful, proud, rude, self-seeking or easily angered; it does not bear grudges or delight in evil, but it rejoices in the truth; it always protects, always trusts, always hopes and always perseveres.

We see all of these characteristics embodied by Jesus as he welcomed women, children, prostitutes and tax collectors into his company; touched and healed lepers, the blind, the lame, the deaf and the demon-possessed; fed the poor and the hungry; had mercy on foreigners, Roman soldiers and synagogue rulers; ate with Pharisees and teachers of the law; and ultimately forgave the very people who incited his crucifixion, even as he hung on the cross.

Much more can be said about the love of God, but the point here is that God is love and his people are to be a people of love (1 John 4:8). In other words, we love because God loves. And our social action is only born out of God if it is born out of love.

The problem is that our culture tends to have a shallow and emaciated understanding of love. Love is more than a good feeling; it's a commitment to seek the welfare of others, even those who are hard to love, and even when love involves sacrifice.

EMBRACING THOSE WHO ARE HARD TO LOVE

Most of us probably don't have many real enemies (we will explore facing opposition in chapter nine), but we all have people we struggle to love for one reason or another. Embracing such people takes patience, humility, intentionality, prayer, repentance and a commitment to seeing the image of God in them.

I once lived next door to someone—I'll call him Adam—who struggled with mental illness and was unemployed. Adam lived on housing subsidies and food stamps, and had no family (he was an immigrant), no money and no support system. For many months, until he was evicted for owing thousands in rent, Adam lived in darkness because he didn't pay his electric bill. Many people tried to help him over the years, but one by one he had burned those bridges. Adam's situation is one of the most hopeless I've encountered in my suburban neighborhood, and being his neighbor was always trying. He depended on just a few of us for most of his needs: toilet paper, soap, cleaning supplies, extra food, rides, money for medicine and so on. But the problem wasn't just how much help Adam needed, but how demanding and manipulative he often was about it.

Adam had a battery-powered lantern and I helped him buy rechargeable batteries so that he could have some light at night. He charged the batteries in my apartment and also regularly stored eggs and other perishables in my fridge. Conflict arose, however, because sometimes when he wanted to charge his batteries or get food from my fridge I wasn't home, which made him angry.

Late one night as I was heading to bed there was banging at my door. Adam was outside calling my name and asking for toilet paper. But it was past midnight and I had run out of patience. I didn't answer the door, the banging continued, and I grew angrier by the moment. After several minutes Adam shuffled over to the widow, peered through the gap in the blinds and called out that he could see I was home. This was the last straw. I stormed over, yanked the front door open, told him it was way too late for this and then slammed it shut in his face.

Adam left, but when I went to bed I couldn't fall asleep. So I prayed, like I often did when I had trouble interacting with him. While his behavior had been inappropriate, I knew that I had reacted out of anger and not love. Adam was often up all night, and I realized that since my light was on, he probably didn't think he was bothering me by asking for toilet paper, which I had given him in the past. What I should have done was give him some toilet paper and explain that this was too late, and in the future he would have to come over by a certain time if he needed anything. Once that boundary was clarified I could start sticking to it. Instead, however, I let my overall tension with Adam boil over into an unloving response. Convicted, I meekly walked over to his apartment with a roll of toilet paper and an apology.

All of us can probably think of people in our lives we find hard to love (just as there are probably people who find us hard to love). Perhaps their values clash with our own, or we find them self-absorbed, intrusive, socially awkward or simply irritating. Or perhaps they struggle with a chronic illness or handicap, whether physical, emotional or psychological, and require more patience and investment from us. As evangelist and teacher Ajith Fernando notes:

> We live in a world whose warped values see weak and unproductive people as unimportant. It seems like a waste of time to invest our energy in such people. But the way a Christian views people is radically different. We know that on the day of judgment, God will not be concerned with our worldly accomplishments. He will look at the fruit of our faith in Jesus Christ— how we treated the hungry, the thirsty, the stranger, the naked, the sick, and the prisoner (see Matthew 25:35-36), people whom our society regards as week and unproductive.[4]

EMBRACING SACRIFICE

Another aspect of godly love that we struggle with is sacrifice. In our pursuit of justice we often avoid speaking of sacrifice because we don't think it's winsome. And it typically isn't. But that's our fault, not God's.

In preparing the way for Jesus, John the Baptist taught that anyone who had two shirts should share one with someone who didn't have any, and those with enough food should do likewise (Luke 3:11). The early church was known for doing this joyfully and powerfully (Acts 2:42-47). Today, we say we care about the poor among us, but how many of us would balk if asked to give up all but one of our coats or computers/tablets or air-conditioning units or cars or most anything else? We'll happily donate things we no longer want (or no longer fit us) to Goodwill or the Salvation Army, but only as it's relatively convenient and doesn't adversely affect our lifestyles. I'm not advocating that we must only own one pair of shoes, for instance, but I am suggesting that we can probably all think of ways we resist or avoid sacrifice.

Our aversion to sacrifice is a weakness within much of the American church today. Just as the cross is central to our faith, sacrifice is an integral part of what it means to be faithful. As Jesus taught, "Whoever wants to be my disciple must deny themselves and take up their cross daily and follow me" (Luke 9:23).

The parable of the good Samaritan provides a compelling model of what it means to sacrificially love our neighbor, even when our neighbor turns out to be an enemy (Luke 10:25-37). In the story a Jewish man is mugged and lies naked and gravely injured along the side of the road. A priest and a Levite both walk by without so much as lifting a finger, but a passing Samaritan stops to help, making himself vulnerable to being mugged in the process. He takes time out of his journey to bandage and care for the victim's wounds, rests him on his own donkey and then brings him to an inn where he covers all the costs of care and lodging.

Like the good Samaritan, engaging faithfully in social action today means being willing to give *sacrificially* of our time, energy, money, belongings, hospitality, comfort, security and the like. In the words of Martin Luther King Jr., the true neighbor "will risk his position, his prestige, and even his life for the welfare of others."[5] Such sacrifice is an expression of our love and belongs at the heart of our faith and social action. Tyler Wigg-Stevenson puts it this way, "This battle is not won by achieving domination over others, but by loving sacrifice on their behalf."[6]

Jesus invites us to experience the joy of embracing sacrificial love for one another, just as he first embraced sacrifice in order to embrace us.

LOVE IS OUR ORIENTATION

What does love in action look like when it comes to our activism today? In some ways, this can be hard to pinpoint. Inward motivations are more complicated than they appear on the surface, and only God can truly discern such matters of the heart (Proverbs 17:3; 1 Corinthians 4:5). Nonetheless, because love runs so counter to our innate selfish tendencies, we can often recognize it when we see it.

One example that comes to mind is my friend Andrew Marin.

I first met Andy when we roomed together at an Urbana Student Missions Conference where we were both speaking. By his own admission Andy grew up as the quintessential alpha male. He went to college on a prestigious baseball scholarship and would be happy watching ESPN's *SportsCenter* 24/7. He was also somewhat homophobic and regularly used words like *gay* or *fag* as casual insults.

The summer after his freshman year in college, however, his three best friends since the age of seven all came out to him, one by one, as being gay or lesbian. In shock, Andy realized that as a conservative Christian he had no idea if and how his values could be reconciled with his friends' sexuality. So he pulled back from them as he struggled with what it could mean to live and love without compromising his beliefs.

Overwhelmed, Andy turned to the Bible and read through it from cover to cover, seeking God's guidance on how to move forward. Then, one day, he sensed God inviting him to think about the situation from his friends' perspectives for a change. What was it like for them to grow up with him as their best friend? What was it like to struggle with their sexual identity while he thoughtlessly referred to them as gays or fags? What was it like to live in fear that if they ever opened up to him he would run away? Which is exactly what he had done.

Convicted, Andy returned to his friends to seek their forgiveness and confess that while he didn't have any answers, he wanted them to remain best friends. Together, they decided to move into Boystown, the neighborhood of Chicago that boasts about sixty gay bars/clubs and around sixty thousand residents, 89 percent of whom self-identify as LGBT.

Thus began a life-changing journey of growth and ministry that continues over a decade later. Andy founded the Marin Foundation (themarinfoundation.org), which actively works to build bridges between the LGBT community and the conservative community, with a focus on evangelical Christians. Now married, he and his wife continue to make their home in Boystown and, in 2009, he wrote a popular book titled *Love Is an Orientation* to share the stories and lessons he has experienced along the way.

While Andy's work has received significant acclamation and positive media coverage, it has also caused controversy and consternation within both the religious and LGBT communities. Many want him to stake out a clear public position on whether he still believes that homosexuality is sinful, which Andy avoids doing in the interest of fostering greater dialogue between both groups.

Andy Marin's story is remarkable for many reasons, one of which is that when things reached a breaking point, both he and his friends persevered in sacrificial love. Instead of turning away from each other in hopelessness, they embraced the deep tensions of continuing to journey together in mutual love and respect. Andy, who describes his childhood self as "the biggest Bible-banging homophobic kid you've ever met,"[7] gave up his more sheltered life to minister in the last place he probably ever dreamed of. Living in the booming center of the LGBT community in Chicago, he overcame the inevitable culture shock to make Boystown his home for building his ministry.

BY OUR LOVE

"A new command I give you," Jesus announced, "Love one another. As I have loved you, so you must love one another. By this everyone will know that you are my disciples, if you love one another" (John 13:34-35).

Christians are known for a lot of things these days—being hypocritical, overly partisan, judgmental—but it's not often for our love.[8] Yet stories like Andrew Marin's and many others give us hope that things can be different and that we can be part of the change.

It's one thing for us to love those who we naturally get along with— anyone can do that, Jesus cautioned (Matthew 5:46-47). The real test is whether even those who disagree with and oppose us can see that we're a loving people. And there's no better opportunity to live this out than through our social action in the public square.

FOR REFLECTION AND APPLICATION

1. We have now moved beyond the old culture war. We are no longer talking about defeating our enemies but about seeking the welfare

of fellow sinners. Take a look at Matthew 5:43-45 and talk about this new paradigm Jesus gives us.

2. In the old paradigm we were motivated by the fear of enemies who might cause us to lose things that are precious to us, things that give us security. In the new paradigm we are motivated by love for fellow sinners, for whom we are willing to sacrifice things that are precious to us, things that give us security. To what extent are we really living in this new paradigm—individually and in our churches?

3. Think of one particular part of your own social action that exasperates you. Is there something about Brother Lawrence's insight that can help you in that area: God "regards not the greatness of the work, but the love with which it is performed"? What is it?

4. Note that we are not called to sacrifice itself but to sacrifice motivated by love for others (1 Corinthians 13:3, 5). There is a kind of sacrifice that is self-seeking and perverse, motivated by a desire to look good and gain applause (Acts 4:32–5:11). Is there a way to check our own motivations for sacrifice?

5. Pray for this to be true in our own lives: "This is how we know what love is: Jesus Christ laid down his life for us. And we ought to lay down our lives for our brothers and sisters" (1 John 3:16).

8

PROPHECY

*For the time will come when people will not put
up with sound doctrine. Instead, to suit their own
desires, they will gather around them a great number
of teachers to say what their itching ears want to hear.*

2 TIMOTHY 4:3

THE CAMPAIGN WAS NOT GOING WELL as the primary election approached.
And I wasn't even facing a competitor until the general election. Yet
our core team was burning out, fundraising was faltering and internal
party opposition to my candidacy persisted. In short, very little was
going according to plan. Struggling to fit in as a candidate and to
juggle all that I needed to know with all the people I needed to win
over, I grew increasingly isolated and discouraged.

As the familiar and lonely weight of depression set in, I began questioning whether I had misread the signs that led me to such an unlikely
grassroots candidacy in the first place. Or maybe this was as far as I
was meant to come and it was time to drop out of the race. Perhaps I
could just quit political activism altogether.

I felt stuck and didn't know what to do or where to turn.

It was during this low point that I received an unexpected package from a prominent progressive blogger in the district. This widely read online activist—who was also openly gay and agnostic—had become an unlikely ally early on in the campaign. There were, after all, plenty of reasons for him to be suspicious of an outspoken evangelical candidate and political rookie coming out of Wheaton College, with its reputation as a bastion of conservative Christianity. But he refused to write me off and eventually became a good friend and one of my strongest supporters.

Opening the package later that night, I found a copy of *Romero*, a film about the life of Oscar Romero, the archbishop of San Salvador from 1977 to 1980. Oscar Romero was a reluctant prophet who lived a relatively quiet and studious life before unexpectedly being appointed archbishop. But his commitment to the gospel meant that he could not stay silent in the face of the widespread injustice and horrific suffering taking place in El Salvador. Archbishop Romero began to preach peacefully but prophetically in support of human rights and against the oppression of the Salvadoran poor. And for that he was martyred. On March 24, 1980, government agents assassinated Romero as he was celebrating the Eucharist rite in a small hospital chapel.

No one was trying to kill me, and the United States is not El Salvador in the 1980s. Nonetheless, our society and politics is very much riddled with injustice and class warfare, and we perpetuate oppression at home and abroad, whether we're talking about the poor trapped in New Orleans after Hurricane Katrina roared through, or the many US-friendly dictators we've propped up in the Middle East and Latin America. (Shortly before he was killed, Archbishop Romero actually wrote a letter to President Jimmy Carter pleading with him—to no avail—to stop shipping weapons to the Salvadoran government, because they were only being used against their own people.)

Accompanying the copy of *Romero*, my agnostic blogger friend included a short note: "You need to unleash your inner Jeremiah. Prophecy is called for today."

He was right. I realized that God was speaking prophetically through him in order to get my attention. Little by little, and like many campaigns, our team had begun to play it safe in order to increase our admittedly slim chances of winning. But faithful political activism—at that time of crumbling climate negotiations, protracted wars, bleak economic struggles and an increasingly toxic health care debate—was not about playing it safe. And it still isn't today.

RECOVERING OUR PROPHETIC WITNESS

Christians often do a poor job of speaking lovingly but prophetically to the problems in ourselves and our society.

Many of our churches are geared toward telling us what we want to hear and helping us feel good about ourselves. A survey exploring why megachurches draw so many worshipers found one of the significant factors to be that the preaching is consistently centered on the numbing and narcissistic message of "unconditional positive regard."[1] In other words, most of the sermons communicate to listeners that "God thinks you're pretty great, and so do we." Sermons on judgment are replaced by sermons on grace, and invitations to sacrifice are supplanted by invitations to comfort. Largely absent is talk about sin— whether personal or societal—especially in forms that hit too close to home, such as anger, greed, materialism and consumerism.

Being prophetic can be uncomfortable for many of us—though some temperaments may find it quite natural—and "unconditional positive regard" is easily more pleasant than "fire and brimstone." But the problem is that it simply isn't the whole truth. And if we're motivated by godly love, then we will ultimately choose what is right over what may seem more agreeable. By avoiding hard but relevant issues, many churches have lost their prophetic witness among their own people and with the surrounding culture.

Prophecy is not necessarily about predicting the future; it's about declaring the word of the Lord through the empowerment of the Holy Spirit. It is about presenting God's truth in relevant ways that challenge the brokenness in our contexts and cultures. This is a weighty and fearful responsibility, and one to be approached with caution and humility.

Prophecy is often for the strengthening, encouragement and comfort of God's people (1 Corinthians 14:3). As we see throughout the Old Testament, however, it can also be about calling out the evil and injustice in society, while casting an alternative vision of God's kingdom of shalom. As such, it's often unpopular and misunderstood.

We celebrate the biblical prophets today but their actual lives were incredibly hard, both because of what God asked them to do as well as the way people treated them in response.

God had Isaiah walk around naked for three years. Ezekiel was told to lie down for 390 consecutive days and cook food over human feces. Hosea had to marry a prostitute and keep taking her back even after she was repeatedly unfaithful. Jeremiah was instructed to wear an actual yoke around his neck, and he was also dropped into a dry well and left for dead. Elijah spent years on the run from Queen Jezebel who had murdered many other Jewish prophets. Daniel was famously hurled into a den full of lions. And Jesus Christ, greatest of all prophets, was executed in the most painful and humiliating way available: by hanging on a cross.

We're not all called to be Old Testament prophets per se—though some, such as Shane Claiborne (among my generation in particular) or Michael Gerson (among political conservatives and Republicans in particular), may serve as modern-day counterparts—but the church is called to engage in prophetic witness and ministry. And we all have a part to play here.

Faithful social action is prophetic. It acknowledges the truth about the broken status quo, even if it's not what people want to hear, and it takes hard but worthwhile steps toward the coming kingdom of God. Facing the brokenness in ourselves and in society is disheartening. It leads us to respond either by grieving and repenting of the status quo or by intentionally ignoring it and returning to our earlier state of numbness, not unlike a dog returning to its vomit. Little surprise then that social action, when properly prophetic, is also typically unpopular and misunderstood.

I offer four further points about our prophetic witness.

First, prophecy isn't just about having strong opinions and a loud voice. Anyone can complain about the way things are, but prophecy also imagines an alternative vision of the way things can and should be. This takes creativity, vision and imagination.

Martin Luther King Jr. didn't have a rant; he had a dream. And he led the way in bringing it into reality. Likewise, Oscar Romero didn't just decry the government; he also opposed violent resistance and advocated for a shared future of peace and dignity for all Salvadorans, poor and rich. Both King and Romero were assassinated, but the kingdom vision they witnessed to lives on and continues to inspire millions of people even today.

Second, being prophetic doesn't necessarily involve being epic or dramatic. There are and will be times when it involves engaging in civil disobedience—as social justice advocate and Sojourners president Jim Wallis has done numerous times—and enduring the fines and jail time that comes along with nonviolently resisting unjust laws. Other times, however, it can simply mean refusing to demonize our enemies and finding tangible ways to show love to those who stand in opposition to us.

During my run for Congress, a campaign adviser suggested that I refer to the incumbent I was running against as my competitor instead of the traditional label of opponent. Though we were competing for the same position with very different ideas and positions, that didn't mean we were opposed to each other as enemies. My competitor wouldn't agree to a meeting or a debate but, since he was a fellow Christian, I wrote him a letter promising to run a civil campaign and committing to pray regularly that God would bless and protect him and his family. He sent a note of thanks in response. This was a minor but meaningful detail, and I'm grateful for the advice I received.

Third, being prophetic requires knowledge and expertise both in theology as well as in the injustices we face today. In order to be prophetic we have to get it right, and in order to get it right we have to be diligent students of the world's problems and God's solutions. The Scriptures warn repeatedly of false prophets, who can be recognized by the fruit they bear. This means that we need Christians who don't just have good intentions but who also know what they're talking about in their field of expertise and how it integrates into their faith.

I think of a former fellow youth group counselor named Si-Cheng. As a math and economics double major in college, Si-Cheng was drawn to the question of what it means to love our neighbors through our economic policies. He wrote a rigorous senior thesis analyzing Ron Sider's classic and prophetic book *Rich Christians in an Age of Hunger*, and then went on to get a masters degree in economics at the renowned University of Chicago. As I write he's now in seminary, where he continues to work through what it means to be faithful and prophetic in key areas of social concern.

Fourth, being prophetic usually involves being on the margins. We speak to the status quo from beyond it, which is another way of saying that we're called to embody the alternative vision that we're advocating. And too often the status quo doesn't even pay attention. But sometimes it does and then starts to change. Consider how surprised and disappointed Jonah was when the Ninevites actually acted on his message, repented of their ways and were spared judgment from God. He was so upset by the success of his mission that he wanted to die (Jonah 4)!

Given these four points, what can it look like to regain our prophetic witness and engage in creative and faithful protest?

"We Love Parkside"

In his seminal book *The Prophetic Imagination*, Walter Brueggemann describes prophetic ministry as "offering an alternative perception of reality and letting people see their own history in the light of

God's freedom and his will for justice." He clarifies that "the issues of God's freedom and his will for justice . . . can be discerned wherever people try to live together and show concern for their shared future and identity."[2]

This is what we're trying to do at Parkside.[3]

Parkside is a low-income apartment complex in the wealthy and largely white suburban Chicago town of Glen Ellyn where over 80 percent of residents are white, the average home costs more than $400,000 and the median household income tops $90,000 per year.[4]

With World Relief resettling refugees in the area since 1979, Parkside has proved an obvious place to house refugees who come from Burma (Myanmar), Nepal, Sudan, Eritrea, Somalia, Iran and similar places.

Parkside is also home to a number of nonrefugee immigrant families, along with an intentional Christian community of just over ten young adults to which I belong. We live among the apartments seeking to serve and learn from our neighbors and each other.

Our complex is always full of life, with kids of all different ethnicities playing together, frequent parties and cookouts throughout the summer, singing and praying from the apartments of the many Christians refugee families, and more cultures, languages and food than anyone can hope for this side of the kingdom.

When people hear about Parkside, they often praise us for being courageous and sacrificial by living here. It's intended as a compliment but we always feel undeserving because the truth is, if we're going to live in the suburbs of Chicago, then Parkside is the place we want to be. We love living here, and so do our neighbors. I didn't realize that pursuing a downwardly mobile lifestyle at Parkside would be a prophetic act as well.

For numerous social and financial reasons, pockets of immigrants and refugees create tensions in wealthy suburbs like Glen Ellyn. In our case, the village of Glen Ellyn had been putting pressure on the owners of Parkside to improve the safety and appearance of the apartment complex.

We do tend to have a lot of litter—a holdover habit from life in the refugee camps—though we've also been working together to keep our complex cleaner. But then officials complained that the grass in parts of the two interior courtyards keeps dying because the kids play together outside too much. They threatened to fine the owners of the complex if they didn't figure out a solution immediately. At their request fencing was installed along almost all of the sidewalks so that kids could no longer step onto the grass.

Matters took a more serious turn, however, when all Parkside residents unexpectedly received a legal notification from the village. This notice included a proposal to include our neighborhood in a new Tax Increment Financing (TIF) district that "may reasonably be expected to result in the displacement of residents."

TIF districts are a (confusing) way for local governments to raise revenue for further developing an area. While originally intended to help improve technically "blighted" neighborhoods, research has demonstrated that TIFs regularly end up harming and displacing low-income communities like Parkside, even when carried out with the best of intentions.[5]

When the village announced a public meeting with staff to discuss the TIF proposal, our intentional community mobilized alongside many of our neighbors. We also asked for support from all our friends and local churches. We hoped for assurances from village officials that they would not harm our community or destroy our apartments. Parkside is our home—some of our neighbors have lived here for twenty years—and we do not want to be sent away. As one of my neighbors from Sudan put it, "I'm a refugee. I've already been displaced once. I don't want to be displaced again."

Upward of three hundred people came out to the public meeting— roughly half from Parkside itself and half from the surrounding areas— to voice support for our neighborhood. About a hundred residents and friends marched the mile from the apartments to downtown Glen Ellyn, carrying homemade signs, waving American flags and cheering, "We Love Parkside" as local reporters followed with their cameras.

Once we met up with the crowd waiting in front of the town hall, a local pastor prayed for the meeting, and then our entire group filed peacefully past the police officers that had been sent out to monitor the situation. On the third floor, we packed out the meeting room, two overflow rooms, and the halls and doorways in between.

Among those gathered were pastors from prominent churches, local teachers, professors from nearby Wheaton College, leaders from World Relief and many others who had become involved at Parkside in one way or another (giving rides, sponsoring new refugee families, volunteering during kids club, etc.). Alone, our neighborhood is easy to write off. The majority of us are poor, do not speak English fluently and lack sociopolitical influence. But with the help of our many friends and supporters, we were able to make our voices heard.

When it came time for public comments—which went late into the night—people of all ages, backgrounds and ethnicities streamed up to the microphone one by one to bear witness to their concerns about the village's plan and share testimonies of life and hope from their relationships at Parkside.

Our message was straightforward. As local pastor Matt Woodley put it, "We're not against economic development, but we won't let the most vulnerable members of our community bear the brunt of our progress."

The village staff listened politely but remained vague in their responses. Over the next couple days, however, we were featured in CBS Chicago, WBBM News Radio, the *Chicago Tribune* and on the cover of the *Daily Herald*, our main suburban newspaper. One reporter told us he had never seen a village meeting quite like that.

Not long after this public meeting, the village president (our mayor) Alex Demos reached out to ask for a meeting with community representatives. He wanted to hear and discuss our concerns himself. The meeting went surprisingly well and a relationship of trust began to grow. At our invitation, President Demos, his family and another trustee came over for dinner with some of our neighbors. Then, completely out of the blue one morning, I got a call that the village board had voted to remove Parkside from the proposed TIF district. They decided that we should get to decide our own future. And they wanted to communicate to everyone that the village valued our community and wanted it to remain part of Glen Ellyn.

Shortly after, we held follow-up meetings with President Demos and other leaders to brainstorm ways to proactively protect and improve the neighborhood. And they gave us an open invitation to negotiate the terms on which we might consider reentering the TIF District.

Throughout this process, we saw lives changed and hearts transformed through relationships with our neighbors. It was a privilege to witness so many local Christians and churches come together across diversities of age, culture, race and socioeconomic status to stand together prophetically for our beautiful but vulnerable neighborhood. As someone involved full-time in activism and advocacy, it was a glimpse into the kingdom of God that I won't soon forget.

For Reflection and Application

1. Our "feel good" churches have not totally abandoned sermons on judgment and sin, but our sermons are largely directed against the sins of those outside the church, preaching judgment that doesn't indict those inside the church. By focusing on "other people's sins" we make ourselves feel pretty good and righteous by comparison. What are some of the sins inside the church that are rarely spoken about?

2. A prophetic voice is not one that condemns other people's sins but indicts us all. It doesn't merely show how the status quo is intolerable but has a vision for how things can be better. And it needs to come from somebody who is—to some extent—already embodying that future reality in how she or he is living right now. If we measure ourselves against all of this, how are we doing in being prophetic voices? Where are we falling short?

3. In our particular area of social action, we have to be "diligent students of the world's problems and God's solutions." How are you being a diligent student of both?

4. Are you involved in a Christian community where the following verse is true? And if so, do you see it as a place you should leave or a place in which you should be a prophetic voice and a prophetic life? "For the time will come when people will not put up with sound doctrine. Instead, to suit their own desires, they will gather around them a great number of teachers to say what their itching ears want to hear" (2 Timothy 4:3).

5. In prophecy, we are called to faithfulness over effectiveness. So, to follow up on the previous question, if you were to decide to stay in order to speak and live prophetically, and you knew in advance that it would change nothing, would you still stay? Explain.

9

OPPOSITION

Consider him who endured such opposition from sinners,
so that you will not grow weary and lose heart.

HEBREWS 12:3

THE CONFERENCE ORGANIZERS KNEW they were taking a risk by inviting me to be one of their plenary speakers.

The New Wilmington Mission Conference takes place every year in Western Pennsylvania and focuses on mobilizing Christians—young adults in particular—to serve on the mission field. Between one and two thousand people pack out the main sessions, which are held outdoors under a big tent.

Although the conference has been running for more than a hundred years, this was their first time addressing the important connections between missions and the environment. As a missionary kid, I'm passionate about this area of overlap, but my hosts weren't sure how the audience might respond. Environmental issues are still viewed by some as being controversial or a distraction.

Thankfully, things seemed to go well and I enjoyed many good interactions with folks who wanted to talk further after the event ended. With one exception.

She was a middle-aged woman and, with a grin that did little to dull her sharp words, she walked up to me and declared that I had been deceived by the devil and was spreading liberal environmental heresies. God was going to come back and destroy the world, she assured those around me, and we need only focus on converting as many people as possible before then. Telling me she would pray for my lost soul, she grabbed me in a tight hug and then walked off, still smiling.

I'm used to opposition but I wasn't sure how to respond to this interaction. At the time I just took a deep breath and went on meeting the others who had come over. But later that night I spent more time thinking and praying over it—being accused of heresy is an unnerving experience.

OPPOSITION IS INEVITABLE

Many of my friends and fellow activists have experienced similar and often harsher confrontations. Some have received threatening messages via phone, email and social media. One was subjected to an actual witch trial in the rural community where she was working. And in a strange coincidence, I once worshiped in a church where the preacher delivered an entire sermon on "modern-day heretics" in which he used one of my friends as the main example.

Facing opposition is a reality for anyone involved in justice work. There's an old saying that God created us in his image, and we've never stopped returning the favor. We like to put God in a box—often based as much on our culture, politics and life experience as on the Bible—and when that's challenged, as social action often does, we can become threatened and react by pushing back.

For instance, there is an older Christian leader who has made it his mission to oppose everything that the Evangelical Environmental Network (EEN) does. He's been our dependable critic for well over a decade now. One of his major gripes is that we advocate for climate action, whereas he has stated that believing in climate change is an insult to a sovereign God who would never let humans do anything *this bad* to the world. (My refugee neighbors and I wonder what he thinks about wars, genocide, slavery and any number of other human-caused horrors.)

When EEN issues a statement, he issues an opposing statement. When EEN launches a new initiative, he sends out fundraising emails to his networks asking for money so that he can continue to counter us. He questions our integrity, refers to us with misleading and polarizing labels and continually tries to stir up controversy and dissension. While we're not his only target, I've come to expect him to be right behind EEN at every step, rallying anyone he can find to oppose our ministry.

Opposition may also flare up from within, and it can be especially hard when it comes from someone we trust. During the first half of my congressional campaign I had trouble finding a good campaign manager. We just didn't have enough money to pay a competitive salary. One of my early supporters, a local progressive activist, volunteered to fill in since she was currently unemployed. I gratefully accepted the offer, but then she stopped showing up at the office and was hard to get in touch with. Shortly after, when we posted a light-hearted campaign video that she fairly deemed as cheesy, she blasted out a mass email to local party leaders attacking me for not being a good enough candidate and calling for my withdrawal. I was stunned. And deeply hurt.

Her email rant was so over the top, however, that it ended up backfiring and party leaders mostly ignored it. Still, because I had trusted her, it took a while for the sting to fade away.[1]

Overcoming Evil with Good

Jesus warns time and again that those who follow him should expect to be opposed, oppressed, persecuted and even killed. And, beginning with his disciples and the early church, countless Christians throughout the years have experienced this prophecy come to pass.

Faithful social action attracts opposition. Most of us don't thrive with conflict, but it's a reality that we have to deal with.

It starts with accepting that not all opposition is bad. Just because we're being opposed doesn't mean that we're on the right side—it could mean just the opposite. As we pursue justice, there will be times we may very well be in the wrong. Then others will need to oppose us in appropriate ways.

Moreover, even bad opposition can have good effects. History shows time and again that heavy persecution has often been accompanied by periods of tremendous growth in the church and advancement of God's kingdom. Opposition can also have a purifying outcome by keeping us honest, careful and dependent on God. Over time I've grown much more precise and thoughtful in the things I say and write because I know that there are people watching and waiting for me to make mistakes.

Potential benefits notwithstanding, how can we respond with grace in the face of hostility?

Jesus taught us to overcome evil with good, to love our enemies and to pray for those who oppose us (Matthew 5:43-48). This runs counter to how we may instinctively want to respond. If someone offends or attacks us then they become our enemy and we need to get them back—it's their fault, not ours!

As the culture wars demonstrates, loving our enemy, however we define *enemy*, is no easier in the public square today than it was on the playground when we were kids. It is, however, very much integral to what it means to follow a Savior who gave his life to rescue us even while we were still in rebellion to him.

Here are five components of a faithful response:

1. Pray. Opposition can cut deep to our core and over time leave us increasingly bitter and vengeful. Prayer grounds us in God and helps us surrender to his will, as Christ showed while awaiting his arrest in the Garden of Gethsemane. It is about submitting to God the opposition we face and the hurt or anger we feel. God is the true judge as well as the source of the love and forgiveness that we need to give, just as we also receive. I've consistently found that prayer makes a critical difference in how I process and respond to opposition.

2. Listen and reflect. Conflict is complicated and blind spots are common—it's dangerous to grow smug or self-righteous. Those who oppose us are likely not completely wrong, and we are rarely completely right. We think we know what's right, but in reality it's often hard to know God's thoughts with certainty. During the American Civil War, both the Union and the Confederacy claimed God for their side. Abraham Lincoln's position on this passionate issue was thoughtful and nuanced, however: "I am not at all concerned about that, for I know the Lord is always on the side of the right. But it is my constant anxiety and prayer that I and this nation should be on the Lord's side."[2] May God give us all this same humility, awareness and discernment.

3. Build bridges. So much conflict and opposition is made worse by a lack of communication and understanding. Instead of pulling back from those who oppose us, we can try to reach out with sincerity and charity, without being patronizing or condescending. Building relationships with those who oppose us is a way to live out the gospel, and sometimes the conflict may even be solved in the process.

This is what happened at Parkside during our campaign against being placed in a TIF district (see chap. 8). Once the village president and another trustee came to have dinner with some of our neighbors, our relationship with the village began to grow in positive and constructive ways. The headline here isn't simply that we fought against the village and won. Rather, it's that we fought with the village and found a way to become friends and work together. More than a tale of victory, it's a story of reconciliation and hope.

Regardless of how well our bridge-building efforts go, however, Christian civility prompts us to privately approach those we disagree with before we go public or hit the blogosphere with our opposition. When the Reverend Mitch Hescox became the president of the Evangelical Environmental Network, one of the first things he did was to reach out to the leader who consistently opposes our work. Many people told him it would be a waste of time—others had reached out through the years to no avail—but Mitch still initiated a dialogue and invested serious effort in trying to build a civil and constructive relationship. As expected, it didn't really going anywhere, but it was still the good and right thing for Mitch to do.

4. Be gracious. All of us are loved by God and created in his image. All of us are also fallen and at the mercy and grace of the redeeming God. In this very real and defining way, we are no different from our enemies. This common image and shared condition enables us to identify with each other, if we are willing, and recognize that we also need mercy and grace from each other.

In the parable of the unmerciful servant (Matthew 18:23-34), Jesus tells the story of a servant who could not pay back a large debt to his master. At the servant's pleading, the master showed mercy and canceled his debt instead of selling his family into slavery. However, this servant then tried to collect on a far smaller debt that a fellow servant owed him. When that fellow servant could not pay up, the first servant ignored his fellow servant's pleas and had him thrown into jail. When the master found out what happened, he had the unmerciful servant locked up and punished until he could pay back the original debt he owed.

Knowing in our hearts how much we daily depend on God's forgiveness should give us every motivation to be forgiving and gracious toward those who oppose or wrong us. In fact, Jesus teaches elsewhere that, as in this parable, our approach toward others is the very measure that God will use to judge us by: "For if you forgive other people when they sin against you, your heavenly Father will also forgive you. But if you do not forgive others their sins, your Father will not forgive your sins" (Matthew 6:14-15).

I struggle with being gracious toward those who have intentionally or maliciously hurt the people I love. As a pastor's kid (PK), I've been pained by the way some members of my parents' church have mistreated and lashed out at them over the years. Most of the congregation has been a blessing, but there have been some very notable and difficult exceptions. Seeing the internal ugliness and politicking firsthand, and yet not being able to do anything about it except smile and remain polite, is one of the reasons that many PKs grow disillusioned and leave the church. While I continue to deal with the hurt from these experiences, I still return to my parents' church when I'm in town. I know that turning my back on those who have hurt my family is not the answer, and I must forgive them just as I desperately need God to continually forgive me for failing him.

5. *Press on.* Opposition can help test and refine us, but it shouldn't keep us from moving forward in the right ways and at the right times. Instead, we should continue to pursue justice in such a way that we can say along with the apostle Paul, "Am I now trying to win the approval of human beings, or of God? Or am I trying to please people? If I were still trying to please people, I would not be a servant of Christ" (Galatians 1:10).

After I had some time to process the angry email that my campaign volunteer had blasted out, I sat down with some advisers and wrote a response. It wasn't so much a defense of my candidacy as it was an expression of sadness that she had become so disappointed by our efforts. I acknowledged my many weaknesses as a candidate but affirmed that, as the nominee in the upcoming election, I would honor my commitment and stay in the race until the end. At the same time I let her know that my door would always be open if she wanted to talk. It was not the easiest email to write—part of me really wanted to call her out for all the ways she had wronged me and the campaign—but it was the right response, so I clicked the "send" button and then focused on moving forward.

A NOTE ON SUFFERING AND PERSECUTION

All this talk about opposition notwithstanding, the truth is that many of us have not and may never suffer from actual persecution. When we face opposition it can be easy to develop a martyr complex and feel sorry for ourselves. I for one often let opposition get to me too easily.

Studying the Bible, reading the stories of actual martyrs through the ages and hearing about the persecuted church today helps to put our troubles into perspective. The opposition we face may be significant and trying but—at least for most of us in the West—it usually pales in comparison to the violent oppression that millions of our brothers and sisters experience all over the world.

A NOTE ON SPIRITUAL OPPRESSION

We often overlook this form of opposition but the Bible is clear that spiritual oppression is a real and dangerous reality: "Our struggle is not against flesh and blood, but against the rulers, against the authorities, against the powers of this dark world and against the spiritual forces of evil in the heavenly realms" (Ephesians 6:12).

Spiritual oppression can be confusing and hard to properly diagnose. It can come in the form of temptations, nightmares, depression, fear or even a sense of darkness and foreboding. But lots of other factors may cause these and other symptoms too. Those of us who tend to be more rational may have a hard time identifying spiritual oppression, while those of us who tend to be more mystical may find it everywhere we look.

For a prolonged period while working on an important project recently, I faced an unusual and overwhelming number of personal challenges and distractions accompanied by deep discouragement. Life can often be hard, so I didn't think much about it. But one day a mentor pulled me aside and said that he thought there might be more going on than I realized. So we started praying specifically against spiritual oppression that might be attacking me and the project. And I asked others to pray in this way as well. Progress never became *easy* but it did finally become possible again.

Though Ephesians 6 doesn't give us specific guidance on how to identify spiritual oppression, it does tell us how to be on our guard:

> Therefore put on the full armor of God, so that when the day of evil comes, you may be able to stand your ground, and after you

have done everything, to stand. Stand firm then, with the belt of truth buckled around your waist, with the breastplate of right-eousness in place, and with your feet fitted with the readiness that comes from the gospel of peace. In addition to all this, take up the shield of faith, with which you can extinguish all the flaming arrows of the evil one. Take the helmet of salvation and the sword of the Spirit, which is the word of God.

And pray in the Spirit on all occasions with all kinds of prayers and requests. With this in mind, be alert and always keep on praying for all the Lord's people. (Ephesians 6:13-18)

THE COST OF OBEDIENCE

The Israeli-Palestinian conflict can be a very heated and controversial topic in the United States. Certain readings of Scripture coupled with a more one-sided understanding of current events have left many American evangelicals strongly supportive of Israel's policies and ac-tions, and less aware of the Palestinian situation (which includes many Palestinian Christians and churches). After all, the Bible teaches that Israel was God's chosen people and we know that Jesus was incarnated as a Middle Eastern Jew.

This is an area where we need to be more theologically balanced and reflective. The worldwide church, not the modern and secular state of Israel, comprises God's chosen people today. Even if biblical Israel still existed as a nation-state, however, that would be no excuse for perpetuating some of the systems of injustice and oppression that exist there today. While Israel certainly has a right to security, Pales-tinians also have a right to justice, and there will be no lasting peace in the region until there is true reconciliation between the two govern-ments and their people. (This is my personal position on the Israeli-Palestinian conflict and does not necessarily represent the people, churches or organizations that I refer to in the rest of this chapter.)

One of my friends, Mae Elise Cannon, serves as an executive leader of a major Christian international development organization focused on responding to the needs of the poor in the Middle East. Much of her work is focused on trying to bring some balance and healing to the highly contentious Israeli-Palestinian conflict.

Mae recalls that when she first got involved in addressing the Israeli-Palestinian conflict, Gary Burge, a New Testament professor at Wheaton College, Illinois, who has written and advocated on this issue for years, warned her that she would face opposition.

He wasn't kidding.

Recently, Mae led an awareness tour called "Hope for the Holy Land," which traveled to churches across America to talk about what's going on in the Middle East.[3] With her were Sami Awad, a prominent Palestinian Christian and advocate for nonviolence, and Lynne Hybels from the highly influential Willow Creek Community Church outside of Chicago. The primary purpose of these events was to foster a view of the Holy Land that is pro-Israeli, pro-Palestinian, pro-peace, pro-justice and ultimately pro-Jesus.

Nonetheless, universally pro-Israeli Christian organizers quickly targeted their tour and took to the blogosphere, talk radio and other venues to denounce their efforts. Mae, Sami and Lynne were labeled several demeaning and inaccurate terms, such as "evangelicals for Hamas," and had to put up with heckling at some of their events. On rare occasions they even received personal threats.

Late one night Mae got a phone call from someone with a gruff voice who wanted to know whether she works with Arabs. The caller went on to talk about God's heart for Israel and to demand whether or not she was on "God's side." He warned her that she'd better be careful because if she turned her back "them Arabs would rip her guts out." The caller said he was only reaching out to warn Mae so she would not be led astray. Then there was the woman who tweeted: "Watch out Mae Cannon, tonight you've met your own worst enemy. I will destroy you."

The opposition spread so effectively in some circles that Mae even received a call from her mother, who was confused and concerned because she had heard somewhere that Mae was traveling with a "Palestinian terrorist" (referring to Sami Awad).

As time goes on Mae and her organization have become more proactive about her safety. So far, there have not been significant threats to her physical well-being, but there have been a couple situations that could have easily gotten out of control. She now has a security protocol and rarely does events alone.

Mae takes all of this in stride, however, and is quick to point out that most of her interactions on the road are very positive, and the opposition she faces doesn't begin to compare to what the apostle Paul and others endured. She says, "There are so many others who have been working on this issue faithfully for decades. They have endured far more pressure, criticism and threats than I can ever imagine." And when she's asked why she continues to persevere on such a tough issue, her response is simple, "I'm not looking for controversy, I'm just trying to be obedient to God's call."[4]

Would that this be true for all of us.

FOR REFLECTION AND APPLICATION

1. Think about some of the opposition you've personally encountered in your social action. How did you feel inside, and how did you react externally to the opposition?

2. Which of the following responses to opposition have you tried: (1) prayer, (2) listening and reflecting, (3) building bridges, (4) being gracious, and (5) pressing on? In what ways were the responses that you did try helpful to you?

3. In facing future opposition, which of the five responses do you feel you need to emphasize more?

4. Social action is a stand against the preservation of misery. As such, "our struggle is not against flesh and blood, but against the rulers, against the authorities, against the powers of this dark world and

against the spiritual forces of evil in the heavenly realms" (Ephesians 6:12). How do we need to incorporate this reality into our thinking?

5. Reflect on this verse and pray through it: "Consider him who endured such opposition from sinners, so that you will not grow weary and lose heart" (Hebrews 12:3).

10

IDOLATRY

*But seek first his kingdom and his righteousness,
and all these things will be given to you as well.*

MATTHEW 6:33

I GREW UP IN SOUTHEAST ASIA, where idol worship was as common and conspicuous in my neighborhood as it was in my bedtime Bible stories.

When Moses was up on the mountain receiving the Ten Commandments from God, the Israelites down in the valley grew impatient and convinced Aaron to melt their jewelry into a golden calf they could worship (Exodus 32). I would read this story at night and then walk past the local Hindu temple on the way to school the next morning. Staring up at the countless ornate idol carvings that adorned their walls and gate, it was easy to imagine what the scene at the base of Mount Sinai might have looked like.

I also had a number of Buddhist friends who had altars and idols displayed prominently around their homes. Their parents took them to the temple regularly, and the scent of burning incense was always on their clothes. Walking by the Buddhist temple compound in my neighborhood, I would often catch a glimpse of the huge and imposing

Buddha statue that took up an entire wall inside their largest building, along with rows of tablets representing various ancestors that people were bowing and praying to. Years later, when I first saw a full-sized pipe organ built into the front wall of a church, it reminded me of that giant Buddha idol.

I never thought idol worship was a good thing, but it was a normal reality all around me.

When I was sixteen my family moved from the overseas mission field to Boston, where my father started pastoring at a Chinese church. Gone were the many temples, which were replaced by churches with steeples. Gone as well were the idols and all the idolatry.

Or so I assumed.

Idols Are Everywhere

The reality is that the United States is just as full of idol worship as any other country in the world. It's just that, for Christians at least, our idols don't look like the Buddha or a golden calf. They are far subtler, though no less harmful.

An idol is anything we are devoted to that ends up replacing or distracting from our fidelity to God. Idols can be found among our possessions, hobbies, relationships, goals and careers. We may never have sacrificed blood and meat offerings to idols, but we still sacrifice time, energy, money and attention to pursue earthly gains. These idols become our masters, and we become their slaves. Or to switch metaphors, idolatry is like a cancer that can spread and take over us before we even realize something is wrong.

For example, we may not have traditional altars around our homes, but many of us have television sets that fill the vacuum. Consider how often TVs functionally become the centerpiece of our living rooms, around which most everything else, including our evenings and weekends, are organized. Can TV shows, movies or video games become idols that detract from our relationship to God?[1] How about our smart phones, tablets and other electronics?

I recently ran an online image search of the word *idol* to remind myself of the specific idols I grew up seeing in my friends' homes and temples. Instead, however, most of the photos that came back were of the highly popular and obsessed-over TV program *American Idol*. Can it get more blatant than that?

Idols are everywhere, and idolatry is an ongoing temptation within each of us. There's a reason Jesus placed so much emphasis on exhorting his listeners to seek first the reign of God in and around them.

Some of us struggle with making money an idol—you cannot serve both God and money, Jesus warned in Matthew 6:24—others struggle with idolizing power, popularity, comfort, security, romance, sex and family. I've even heard of a pastor commenting that one of the biggest problems he sees in his wealthy suburban community is the idolatry of children.

In his convicting book *Gods at War*, pastor Kyle Idleman asserts

Idolatry isn't just one of many sins; rather it's the one great sin that all others come from. So if you start scratching at whatever struggle you're dealing with, eventually you'll find that underneath it is a false god. Until that god is dethroned, and the Lord God takes his rightful place, you will not have victory.[2]

IDOLATROUS ACTIVISM

Many of our idols are not inherently bad, and some of them even start out as blessings or callings from God. But they quickly turn into idols when we put our trust in the gift instead of the Giver or when we find our value in the mission instead of the Master.

This includes our social action, as Idleman notes later in his book:

You could be serving something that is in itself, very commendable. . . . It could be a worthy cause. You could even be feeding the hungry and healing the sick. All of those are good things. The problem is that the instant something takes the place of God, the moment it becomes an end in itself rather than something to lay at God's throne, it becomes an idol.[3]

Let's assume, as Idleman does, that we start out in social action with only good intentions. We want the world to change for the better. We want good things like justice and peace for ourselves and for those around us. So, we engage in activism and advocacy to pursue these noble goals.

We set out to do God's work and build his kingdom, but too often our egos and personalities get in the way, and we end up promoting ourselves and building our own reputation. We start to put our hope in human ability and effort rather than ultimately looking to God. We begin to trust in our own social action to change the world rather than trusting in God. We buy into the lie that we're achieving our vision for the world with our own resources and strategies—especially when we experience signs of progress—instead of acknowledging our dependence on God's strength and provision in order to faithfully carry out his work. Before long, we've turned social action into an idol and have begun exalting ourselves, others or even the cause above God.

Faithful social action involves continuously recognizing and dealing with the false idols that so easily creep into our social action.

Jesus at the Center

The first step toward dealing with idolatry is to admit that we have a problem. Honest and probing questions can help us sort through our lives and specifically our social action to root out things that have or are becoming idols.

What do I experience longings for? What do I daydream about or fill my down time with? Where do I turn when I get discouraged? What disappoints me? What makes me anxious? What am I afraid of losing or going without?

Our respective answers to these and other similar questions are not automatically idols. But they are usually areas to watch closely.

The second step is to submit our idols to God and intentionally pursue the lifelong discipline of keeping Jesus at the center of everything. This involves both cutting off unhealthy attachment to our idols as well as growing our relationship with Christ. The solution to idolatry is ultimately to fix our eyes on Jesus, the author and perfecter of our faith (Hebrews 12:2). If Jesus is the center, everything else falls into its proper place.

What can this look like practically?

The idols connected to our social action can be divided into two broad categories: (1) idols that *distract or discourage us from* activism, and (2) idols that *arise from and feed into* our activism.

I addressed some of the reasons we avoid social action—the first category—in the first section of this book (particularly chap. 3), though there are some idols such as apathy that I haven't addressed in great depth. (If you're making the effort to read this book, then apathy is probably not your main struggle.)

The rest of this chapter will focus on the second category—idols that often result from engaging in social action, which in some ways is even more sinister and subversive than the first. I've further organized it into three distinct though interconnected subcategories: the traps of idolizing ourselves, idolizing others and idolizing the cause.

A significant part of the answer to each of these traps has to do with our contemplative life, our observance of the sabbath and our grounding in community, which are topics of upcoming chapters. With that in mind, here are some other steps and disciplines that can help address the idols in our social action.

IDOLIZING OURSELVES

There's a fine line between empowerment and idolatry. We idolize ourselves when we subconsciously begin to act as if the world centers on and revolves around ourselves. Or when we start believing that we can save the world. Not only is this false, it's also dangerous, as Tyler Wigg-Stevenson notes: "A generation of Christians that thinks it is called to save the world is a generation firing on the fuel of false hopes. It is signing up for exhaustion and disillusioned burnout."[4]

The church today is plagued with pride, narcissism and selfish ambition. We all face this at varying levels, and some personality types struggle more than others here. Many strong leaders are effective because they have confident, dominant and aggressive personalities. The downside is that this also makes them more likely to become hostile and egotistical.

This plays out all the time in our activism and advocacy, as leaders jostle for the limelight and act in very un-Christian ways in order to get or stay ahead. What A. W. Tozer wrote many years ago remains just as true today:

> Egotism, exhibitionism, self-promotion, are strangely tolerated in Christian leaders even in circles of impeccable orthodoxy. . . . I trust it is not a cynical observation to say that they appear these days to be a requisite for popularity in some sections of the Church visible. Promoting self under the guise of promoting Christ is currently so common as to excite little notice.[5]

I speak at a number of Christian conferences every year and have grown to dread the ego and comparison games that often take place when a bunch of activists, authors, pastors and other leaders converge in the same room. The unspoken and even subconscious process of developing a social hierarchy creeps in with casual name-dropping, conversations about the book contracts we have, the boards we sit on, the awards we've received and anything else that makes us appear important and impressive. I know this because I catch myself doing it. It doesn't mean we don't truly care about one another or that these aren't legitimate things to chat about. Rather, it's the way we talk about them and the motivation within our hearts that can so easily become twisted and harmful. It's really hard to completely avoid comparing and competing with each other.

In their very honest and helpful book, *Renovation of the Church*, copastors Kent Carlson and Mike Lueken write about facing this problem among fellow church leaders:

> It's the way the world works. The same dynamic occurs in a wolf pack. Only one wolf is the alpha male; everyone else falls in line. Still, all of us knew quite well that Jesus taught us that we were to do it a bit differently. If we wanted to become great, we must be a servant, and if we wanted to be first, we must be the slave of all (Mark 10:43-44).[6]

We can all think of many other examples of selfish ambition in the church. I recently came across the website of a ministry that seemed to be mostly about glorifying its executive director, whose glamour shots and list of accolades and accomplishments were spread all over the home page and throughout many of the subpages. But to be honest, we probably need look no further than in our own hearts. In this age of personal websites, social media, blogging platforms and other intense branding and marketing, it's hard to engage in the public square without becoming self-promotional and self-seeking.

How can we navigate this field of ego landmines?

John the Baptist is a great example of someone who had every reason to struggle with egotism and selfish ambition, and yet by all accounts stayed humble and grounded. John was a renowned celebrity during his ministry days. Crowds of people flocked to hear him speak, and many of them were baptized. Even the religious and political rulers of the day were intrigued and intimidated by him. No one was more popular or influential at that time than John the Baptist. No one, that is, until Jesus came on the scene and started to eclipse him.

Naturally, John's disciples grew concerned about this and approached him saying, "Rabbi, that man who was with you on the other side of the Jordan—the one you testified about—look, he is baptizing, and everyone is going to him" (John 3:26).

If I were John the Baptist, I could easily hear myself grumbling about how I helped this upstart Jesus guy launch his ministry by baptizing and endorsing him, and now he's competing with my program and stealing my audience. But John's reply was both self-aware and God-focused:

> A person can receive only what is given them from heaven. You yourselves can testify that I said, "I am not the Messiah but am sent ahead of him." The bride belongs to the bridegroom. The friend who attends the bridegroom waits and listens for him, and is full of joy when he hears the bridegroom's voice. That joy is mine, and it is now complete. He must become greater; I must become less. (John 3:27-30)

"He must become greater; I must become less." This is a quote we hear and affirm a lot, but it can be very hard to live into fully. As we fix our eyes on Jesus, here are three intentional practices that can help keep us from idolizing ourselves:

Serve in hidden ways. Social action can be a very visible endeavor and sometimes we risk getting intoxicated on all the attention. I've found it valuable to always be involved in something where the attention is not on me and I can serve quietly in the background. At times this has been putting together slides of song lyrics for worship services, planting a garden or helping refugee neighbors fill out (tedious) official paperwork. The key is to pursue things that don't feed our egos.

Do things in teams. Teams help smooth out our rough edges, hold us accountable and keep our egos in check. Healthy teams can help prevent any one person from becoming too controlling or taking all the credit. Over the years I've been blessed to work on a number of tight-knit teams that trust each other and share both the workload and any achievements. On a healthy team the mission is bigger than any individual, and team members are intentional about supporting and encouraging one another.

Seek the welfare of others. "Do nothing out of selfish ambition or vain conceit," the apostle Paul writes in Philippians 2:3-4. "Rather, in humility value others above yourselves, not looking to your own interests but each of you to the interests of the others." For several months I got to represent my church in an interdenominational meeting of local pastors who were coming together to find ways that their individual churches could start partnering as a larger body to reach the surrounding community. It was an inspiring experience as I sat at the table and listened to the group of pastors encourage, support and pray for one another. They found specific projects that their congregations could collaborate on and even came together around a sermon series that they took turns preaching from one another's pulpits. What a great example of how we can serve rather than compete with one another.

These are some of the intentional steps we can take to resist the cancer of self-idolatry in Christian leadership, ministry and social action. There are undoubtedly others. And sometimes seemingly random circumstances can also conspire to keep us humble.

I once spoke at a major conference where my workshop was scheduled for a location in a completely different building about a mile away from the main venue. On top of that hurdle, they set me up in a banquet hall that seated over a thousand people. It was huge. And empty. The first workshop I gave attracted about fifty people, which I thought was okay given the circumstances. But it sure felt vacant in that cavernous room.

Between my first and second workshop, however, they scheduled a very popular author to speak in the same hall. I watched in amazement as well over a thousand people poured in to hear this other speaker. They filled every chair and sat along the aisles and up the staircases. As soon as he was done the moderator got up and plugged my upcoming workshop, which was kind of her, but did nothing to stem the wave of people that poured out of the room headed for other sessions. By the time things settled down, I had about twenty-five people left for my second round. No ego boost there!

IDOLIZING OTHERS

Sometimes the problem is less that we're tempted to idolize ourselves and more that we're drawn toward idolizing the leaders we respect and admire. It's good to know our tendencies here.

We have an infatuation with celebrities in our culture, and it regularly spills over into the church. This idolatry manifests itself in numerous ways and extends to include Christian musicians, preachers, politicians, actors, authors and activists. We've all heard the screaming and cheering that erupts when a famous worship band takes the stage at a concert. I've never been comfortable with such adulation. It's one thing to respect and admire people for their talents or efforts, but it's another thing to fawn over them when we should instead be focused on worshiping God.

When it comes to social action, it's also easy to idolize historical figures like Martin Luther King Jr., Mother Teresa, William Wilberforce and others. The problem occurs when we go from being inspired by their example to idealizing them as people who did or can do no wrong. In doing so we place our hopes and trust in another broken human being, which only leads to disappointment. This is partly why so many of us struggle with cynicism through the years. We need leaders we look up to and respect—but not leaders we worship.

We're all looking for a Messiah and sometimes we foolishly turn to another human being to fulfill this role. As we fix our eyes on Jesus, we remember that we're all made from dust, our bodies will all return to dust once we die, and we all poop and put our pants on one leg at a time. Instead of idolizing another person, no matter how compelling or capable that person is, we place our hope and trust in Christ, who is the only true Savior.

One practical way that we can do this is to seek out mentors, advisers and spiritual guides based not on their prominence but on their faithfulness. Instead of pursuing a relationship with the most popular professor, pastor or leader within our reach, what would it look like to seek out those who are serving faithfully but do not receive as much recognition and are not making a big deal about it? In doing so we'll find that we've been overlooking a lot of people who stand to teach us a great deal. At the end of the day, the question we should be asking about those we look up to is whether they ultimately point us to themselves or to Jesus.

Diane Swierenga (formerly Diane Garvin) has been one of my mentors and prayer warriors for over ten years. Originally, Diane and her husband, John, planned on being church planters overseas. After years of hard work and careful saving, their mission agency commissioned them to serve in Trinidad. Only six months into their stay, however, John was involved in a serious car accident that killed a good friend and required him to be flown back to the United States for medical treatment. Numerous surgeries and much healing later, they eventually made it back overseas, this time to South Africa. But once again they had to return unexpectedly when John developed major health issues.

Settling into the Chicago area in 1988, Diane started working at the Billy Graham Center at Wheaton College while John became involved in numerous church and community ministries. As John's health worsened throughout the years, Diane remained by his side, caring faithfully for him until he passed away in 2002.

I met Diane early on during my freshman year at Wheaton in 2003. She ran the Billy Graham Scholarship Program, which supports church leaders from the United States and around the world who need financial assistance to study at the graduate school. And until she retired in 2013, she also coordinated a phone bank for the Billy Graham Evangelistic Association, which takes calls from viewers who dial the hotline number on their screens during reruns of Billy Graham Crusades.

My father had received research funding through this Billy Graham Scholarship Program a number of years back, and Diane remembered me when we ran into each other on campus (though I had grown a lot since then!). Recognizing that I was far from home, she quickly took me in as her "Wheaton son." Since then I've spent countless hours at her house hanging out with friends, watching movies, eating good food, doing laundry, growing a vegetable garden and much more. It's truly a home away from home for me.

Life has not been easy for Diane. She's been through many trials and disappointments, and has experienced much grief and pain. But through it all she has continued to persevere faithfully in seeking and serving God, often in quiet and hidden ways. Diane is a warm and caring person who goes out of her way to show care for those in her path. Through her many roles and relationships, Diane has unassumingly blessed, empowered and prayed with countless students, neighbors, colleagues and others like me. Her enduring trust in and devotion to God, and her life of sacrificial service, has taught me a lot about what it means to wait on and follow Jesus in a broken world.

IDOLIZING THE CAUSE

Finally, when God places an issue on our hearts, it's all too easy to become so immersed in fighting for the cause that it becomes our obsession and starts to usurp God's place in our lives.

This is the idol I tend to struggle with the most. We all long for meaning and purpose, and throwing ourselves into a cause can help realize some of this. But there's a fine line between finding our value in God and finding our value in the work he has called us to do. There is great value to work, and it's a good feeling to be doing what we were created for, but it should always build up and not distract from our relationship with God.

I recognize this problem in my life when I lose the sabbath, grow too restless to appreciate solitude, become obsessive about checking my email and social media accounts, and can't find the time for spiritual contemplation that isn't directly related to the issues I'm working on. Instead of pouring my life out in service to God, I start to live, breathe, dream and feed off the cause. I even make excuses that all of this sacrificing is necessary because otherwise the mission will fail without me. That's ridiculous. The truth is that I don't know what I would do without the cause. This attitude can make me an especially effective activist, at least in the short run, but it also makes me a disobedient disciple. And that tradeoff is never worth it.

Like any of our other signature idols, this is an unsustainable relationship that will inevitably end in disappointment. When we idolize a cause, we replace faithfulness with effectiveness as our goal, and our tactics can go downhill fast. We eventually burn out or otherwise reach the point where we feel overwhelmed, discouraged and lost. Rather than longing for the success of our cause, we can embrace and cultivate a longing for God and for God's reign to be consummated over all things. This orientation will always lead us toward hope.

In other words, and at the risk of being annoyingly repetitive in this chapter, the solution to idolizing the cause is to fix our eyes on Jesus and cultivate our relationship with him through spiritual disciplines such as prayer, fasting (particularly fasting from technology and communication), retreats and observing the sabbath.

A Lifelong Jesus-Centered Activist

I recently participated in a retirement gala for Ron Sider, an author, professor and founder of Evangelicals for Social Action (ESA).

As usual, I went somewhat apprehensive of the comparison game that I've come to expect among Christian leaders, but was pleasantly relieved to find that it just didn't seem to be as much of an issue here. A lot of this probably had to do with Ron and the personal example he has set through the years as an influential evangelical leader who seems to have avoided becoming self-important or pretentious.

Just to give you an idea of what I mean by this, the dinner celebration took place in the banquet hall of a nice hotel, but the dress code was "Ron Sider casual: wear your thrift store finest" because Ron has become famous for living—and dressing—simply.

It was a grand party that brought together a few hundred of Ron's friends and colleagues from over four decades of service at ESA, many of whom are well known leaders themselves. At the end of the dinner a handful of close associates roasted Ron, sharing numerous hilarious (and mostly true) memories about his life and ministry.

It was a blast from start to finish. But what struck me the most was how Jesus-centered the whole event was, and how everyone's stories pointed to how Jesus-centered Ron's lifelong ministry had been. This characteristic also comes through in his writing. Though one of the most visible Christian leaders involved in social action, one of Ron's books is titled *I Am Not a Social Activist: Making Jesus the Agenda.*

Without making the mistake of idealizing Ron Sider, I believe that he serves as a positive example of someone who has been able to faithfully pursue social justice without falling into the trap of idolizing himself, idolizing others or idolizing the cause. Whatever weaknesses he may also have, Ron seems to have stayed true to this basic belief in both word and deed over the last forty years: what distinguishes our Christian activism from every other kind of social action is not just how we do it but why we do it: for Christ and *his* kingdom.

For Reflection and Application

1. This chapter urges us to examine our lives to see if there are things that have become or are becoming idols to us. The following questions may be helpful to identify them: What do I experience longings for? What do I daydream about or fill my down time with? Where do I turn when I get discouraged? What disappoints me? What makes me anxious? What am I afraid of losing or going without? Talk with your group about this.

2. What are some idols that distract or discourage us from activism?

3. What are some idols that arise from and feed into our activism?

4. Have you tried—or are you willing to try—any of the following antidotes to idolatry? Serve in hidden ways. Do things in teams. Seek the welfare of others. Seek an unrecognized but faithful

mentor. Pray. Fast from food. Fast from technology. Go on a retreat. Observe the sabbath. Explain.

5. Having identified our idols, ask the Lord to help you to "seek first his kingdom and his righteousness" (Matthew 6:33).

11

REPENTANCE

My grace is sufficient for you, for my
power is made perfect in weakness.

2 CORINTHIANS 12:9

SOME SAY THAT SLAVERY IS AMERICA'S ORIGINAL SIN, though surely our treatment of Native American tribes is part of this terrible legacy as well.

Despite the passage of time, and without downplaying the significant progress that has been made, racial tension and discrimination is still rampant throughout the country. Slavery may be outlawed, but its effects have not been erased. Even what Martin Luther King Jr. said about the church decades ago remains largely true today: 11 a.m. on Sunday is the most segregated hour in America.

When I moved to the United States as a teenager, I was vaguely aware of slavery and the civil rights movement, but mostly from a historical angle. I knew about what had happened but thought everything was more or less in the past. One of the longest-lasting culture shocks I had was coming to terms with the deep ongoing racial tensions and injustices that permeate our society to this day. In many ways I'm still dealing with this reality.

Growing up in the highly diverse nation of Singapore, I had friends from many different races and ethnicities, and we all got along well with one another. Things weren't perfect, but we were blessed not to have to deal with the dark and heavy heritage of slavery and segregation. Coming from this background, I confess that for some time I struggled to understand why so much baggage and tension still exists. I don't wonder anymore.

My awakening happened one evening a few years after college, while I was hanging out with some friends and former roommates. We decided to head into Chicago to one of our favorite Mexican restaurants near where we used to live. Carpooling into the city that rainy night, we were discussing, ironically, as it turns out, the recent passage of harsh immigration laws in Arizona, and the anticipation that the new legislation would entrench racial profiling and increase harassment of both documented and undocumented minorities.

Because the highway was jammed with traffic due to construction, we turned down a local road that we hoped would be faster. A few minutes went by when, suddenly, flashing lights appeared behind us and we were pulled over by officers from a local police department.

The officers initially gave no reason for the traffic stop and ignored our requests for them to tell us why we were pulled over. Instead, they ordered us out of our car, lined us up against their squad cars and searched our bodies, removing everything in our pockets. Our vehicle was searched as well. The whole process took a while, and when nothing illegal was found, one of the officers explained that we were pulled over because we "looked Latino," and they were experiencing problems with Latinos trafficking drugs along that road.

I couldn't believe my ears. Not that I might be mistaken for being Hispanic—being biracial and dark-haired it happens occasionally—but that the officer would so blatantly admit to racial profiling and expect us to be okay with it.

They returned our licenses, thanked us for cooperating and let us go. When I asked for the officers' badge numbers so I could follow up on the incident, they ended up writing us a spurious ticket for not wearing seatbelts.

The point of this incident is not the inconvenience and humiliation of a roadside stop and search of law-abiding citizens engaged in no illicit activity on what was meant to be a pleasant night out. The point is also not to protest the minor injustice of a bogus traffic ticket, which a judge quickly dismissed later in court. (We also filed an official complaint with the police department, but they don't release the findings of internal investigations, so we have no way of knowing if anyone was ever disciplined.)

The point is that for one night I experienced a relatively mild taste of the racial profiling and discrimination that millions of people of color still experience every day in America. It made racial tensions and baggage real to me in a small but personally significant way. I grew up always trusting law enforcement, but this incident opened my eyes to the corruption that occurs even among some of those commissioned to serve and protect us. It left me feeling afraid, angry and deeply disillusioned.

More than anything, however, it caused me to lament. It made me face up—in a more personal way than ever before—to our sinful national heritage on racial issues and the way we still often treat each other differently because of the color of our skin. It led me to grieve over the small injustice I experienced and to begin to extend that grief to those whose families and communities that have suffered from racial and ethnic discrimination for generations.

Broken People in a Broken World

The world is broken in part because we are broken.

This means that we often share some of the responsibility for causing or perpetuating the very problems that we're trying to address. Our lifestyles and economies are sustained largely by exploitative and unsustainable systems. We use energy generated from wantonly destructive methods, we eat food that comes from inhumane practices, and we wear clothes made using unjust labor conditions. The list goes on.

Our brokenness also means that in attempting to fix such problems, we will likely make further mistakes along the way. Good intentions are important, but they don't prevent us from causing inadvertent harm. We may zealously intervene to do things for others without giving them the dignity of choice or the tools to create self-sufficiency; we may take too little time to listen and learn before we act—especially in crosscultural settings—and end up causing offense or harm; we may become so driven toward our goals that we end up ignoring, neglecting or mistreating the people around us. This list could go on as well.

As such, faithful social action requires an ongoing posture and practice of repentance, which is a process that first begins with lament.

RECOVERING LAMENT

Lament is a biblical response to injustice that runs through the Scriptures, particularly in the Psalms, Prophets and of course the book of Lamentations. In the Gospels we read that Jesus lamented over Jerusalem for its stubborn disobedience and rejection of God's messengers all the way up to himself: "Jerusalem, Jerusalem, you who kill the prophets and stone those sent to you, how often I have longed to gather your children together, as a hen gathers her chicks under her wings, and you were not willing" (Matthew 23:37; Luke 13:34).

To lament in activism is to express sorrow, mourning and regret over the brokenness around us. It's a necessary though often neglected part of acknowledging and responding to injustice. Professor and activist Soong-Chan Rah writes about the need for and lack of lament today:

> The typical American church fails to engage lament. Several different studies have shown that our liturgies, our hymnals, and our worship songs lack lament while disproportionately over-emphasizing triumphalist songs of praise. Our worship does

not reflect the balance of praise and lament found in the Scripture. The American church avoids lament. Even when lament is found, it is often a quick stop on our trajectory towards victorious praise psalms. We move quickly away from lament to praise because we want a nice, neatly wrapped narrative that meets our worldview.[1]

Lament is the first step toward both repentance and healing. That's why candlelight vigils, prayer services and other communal gatherings are so important in the wake of injustices and tragedies such as mining accidents or school shootings. They provide a venue for lamentation and enable us to face and deal with harsh realities together, instead of hiding our grief or burying our pain in isolation. They also help ready us to take responsibility for our part in the problems, as well as our role in the costly struggle toward justice and reconciliation that always lies ahead.

RECOVERING REPENTANCE

Lamenting my experience with racial profiling also led me to repentance, particularly for how I had previously underrated the severity and prevalence of racial injustice. I simply hadn't encountered systemic racial injustice in the United States yet, and didn't realize how much of an ongoing problem it remains. As a result I didn't take an active stand on it and instead grew impatient with some of my friends who did.

Repentance is an integral part of our social action today. It calls us to lament our mistakes along with the brokenness around us and then make a conscious decision to turn away from past sin and toward future obedience. Repentance is about more than apologizing. It's a commitment to doing things differently as we move forward. And it's a critical step in the journey of healing and reconciliation with those we have wronged or with those who have wronged us.

A couple specific examples come to mind.

Toward the end of my campaign, our team was given a directory of mailing addresses of faculty and staff at a nearby college. It was technically a private listing, but we also knew it was frequently used for a variety of unofficial and unsanctioned mailings. Not thinking it was a big deal, and eager to reach more potential voters with our message, we sent out a targeted campaign mailing to many of the people in that directory.

It was probably one of our most effective mailings, but it also created a stir. One of the college recipients guessed that we might have used the directory to confirm her address and called into the campaign office angrily threatening legal action and chewing out our poor staffer who happened to answer the phone.

There must have been other complaints because I later met with one of the college's senior administrators who asked me to send the college a formal apology letter for how our campaign had misused their directory. On one hand I knew they were making a bigger deal than usual out of this—many people misuse the campus directory—and that was disappointing. But on the other hand I felt embarrassed because I knew it was our fault and it shouldn't have happened. So I wrote a sincere apology letter and instructed our campaign not to use directories like that for future mailings. The college administration accepted my letter and graciously affirmed that they would put this issue to rest and keep it from clouding our relationship moving forward.

In another instance I served as a press contact for our community effort to protect the Parkside apartments from possible redevelopment (see chap. 8). I spoke to a number of reporters about our concerns and was excited to see how much press coverage we received. The radio stories and newspaper articles helped focus a lot of public attention on our cause.

While reading one of the articles, however, my heart sank as I realized that one of my quotes had been shortened and ended up portraying some of our government officials in an unfair light. My edited comment made them sound heartless. Mortified, I quickly scheduled a meeting with the village manager, apologized for the inaccuracy and committed to being more careful in future interviews.

CORPORATE REPENTANCE

Repentance doesn't always just happen on a personal level, as the previous two examples describe. Sometimes it's also needed on a corporate level.

In 2008 Prime Minster Kevin Rudd of Australia delivered a formal apology in parliament, broadcast live across the nation, for the years of abuse and suffering inflicted by successive governments on the indigenous Aboriginal populations. This long overdue apology was well received across Australia, though some argue that it fell short of true repentance because it was not accompanied by any actual restitution.

At their annual convention in 1995 the Southern Baptists, the largest Protestant denomination in the United States, finally formally renounced its racist roots and apologized for its past support of slavery, segregation and racial discrimination. More than just an apology, however, the convention also committed to intentionally valuing and actively fostering greater racial diversity among their members and leaders. While they still have a ways to go, in 2012 the Southern Baptist Convention elected Fred Luter Jr. as its first African American president.

On a more personal note, I currently serve as the board chair of the Au Sable Institute, a Christian environmental studies organization based out of one of the most beautiful places in the United States—northern Michigan. Established in the 1970s, Au Sable was foundational in building up the creation care movement and has a rich heritage of inspiring and educating people to serve and protect God's earth.

In the early 2000s, however, the institute spiraled into a financial crisis. The long-time executive director left, and those who remained struggled to stabilize things. It got so bad that at one point the board sent out a public letter notifying everyone that Au Sable would likely shut down in the near future. This caused alarm among our constituents, who rallied and helped to save the institute, though a great deal of trust was lost along the way.

Some years down the road now, things are once again looking up for Au Sable. Our finances are stable, fundraising is growing, enrollment for our courses and programs is healthy and we're blessed with strong staff and board teams that work well together.

Recently, however, we realized that no one had ever apologized to our constituents for some of the ways things were handled during the crisis period that they went through. Part of the reason for this is that there has since been complete turnover on the board—none of us serving today were around back when things came close to falling apart. Despite this, however, we recognize that part of the process of building back trust involves accepting responsibility for past mistakes and doing our part in the present to corporately repent for the hurt that had been done.

It's Okay to Make Mistakes

Whether it's at the personal or corporate level, we're going to make mistakes as we fight for justice. It's inevitable.

It's good to learn from the errors that others make, but we also do well to accept that we will make our own share of mistakes along the way. It's part of being broken people in a broken world, and it's also part of how we gain wisdom and experience. We can't let our fear of messing up paralyze and prevent us from persevering in social action.

At the end of the day, how we deal with our mistakes is most important. Will we double down and try to hide our errors in order to save face? Or will we take responsibility for our actions—or the actions of others who represent us—and humbly pursue repentance?

For Reflection and Application

1. Have you personally suffered from racial and ethnic discrimination? How real is this injustice to your family? To your friends? To your church?

2. Have you ever been part of communal lament, for example, a candlelight vigil or prayer service in the wake of some injustice or tragedy? How did it affect you?

3. Is lament a frequent or rare part of your church's life? Is there a balance between giving thanks to God for the inherently good structures of society that preserve morality, family and freedom with lament for the inherently evil structures of society that preserve misery? If not, why do you think there is an imbalance, and how does it affect the life of your church?

4. What is one form of systemic injustice in which you feel implicated? Having recognized that you are a responsible party in the perpetuation of this injustice, how have you moved from an intellectual admission of this fact to actual lament and repentance?

5. We are all part of the problems we are addressing, so reflect on this verse and spend some time in prayer: "My grace is sufficient for you, for my power is made perfect in weakness" (2 Corinthians 12:9).

12

SABBATH

Be still and know that I am God;
I will be exalted among the nations,
I will be exalted in the earth.

PSALM 46:10

WE'RE STRIVING SO HARD TO CHANGE THE WORLD that we rarely feel like we can pause to rest. But faithful social action involves practicing the sabbath. How can we live into this gift and discipline in a world that never stops?

I've made a serious commitment to practice the sabbath now, but it hasn't always been this way. Even though I attended a Christian college, taking a special day of rest was something that rarely factored into our campus culture. And it was nearly impossible because the academics were rigorous and we often had tests or assignments due early in the week. Most of my weekends were split tightly between serving in various ministries at my local church, which the college encouraged us to do, and catching up on my studies.

After graduating from college I jumped straight into full-time activism and started working for a Christian nonprofit organization. A lot of our public ministry happened in churches on the weekends, and we rarely took another day off during the rest of the workweek. There was always so much to do, so many emails to reply to and never enough hours in the day to get everything done. Sound familiar?

Then I took on my first book project and the margins grew even tighter. Every moment of every day was spent either keeping up with my job or writing frantically to meet my contractual deadlines. I occasionally had to pull all-nighters while in college, but this was the first time I resorted to chugging energy drinks to stay focused and awake. This lifestyle started to take a toll on my health, but I pushed on, convincing myself that once the book was finished things would settle back down again.

They didn't.

As the writing wrapped up, I became part of an effort to launch a grassroots activist network called "Renewal: Students Caring for Creation," which would organize and resource creation care efforts on campuses across the United States and Canada. This new organization, which I wrote about in *Green Revolution*, had been a personal dream coming out of my college experience, and I eagerly accepted an offer to serve on staff as one of the co-coordinators. Along with this new position came new responsibilities and new demands, and the pace of life continued to ramp up.

Outwardly, I appeared to be enjoying a great deal of success. Still in my early twenties, I was already a published author and was leading a growing national ministry. I loved the work God had given me and found it very meaningful. Inwardly, however, I was also growing increasingly weary and overextended. Ironically, my work advocating for sustainability had itself become unsustainable.

Signs of Burnout

Things came to a head during our cross-country campus tour. There are more than one hundred Christian colleges and universities across North America that are part of the Council for Christian Colleges and Universities (CCCU), and my colleague and I attempted to visit over thirty of them in a single semester. The goal was to introduce Renewal, survey the creation care efforts happening on the ground and build relationships with key leaders.

We planned to start in San Diego, make our way up to Seattle, cross the Canadian border into Vancouver, swing through much of the Midwest and Northeast, and dip into some of the Southern states at the end. To save on costs, we would crash with students in their dorms and eat as their guests in the cafeterias. We should have realized that our itinerary was far too ambitious to be healthy, but we felt young and invincible, and didn't have a good sense of personal limitations yet. So we forged ahead.

The tour was equally fruitful and exhausting. We learned a lot about the good environmental efforts being pioneered on campuses across the United States and Canada, and were able to connect with and encourage many remarkable student leaders and groups. But it turns out that sleeping on grungy dorm room couches night after night, surrounded by someone else's dirty laundry and leftover pizza just isn't very restful in the long run. We had few breaks and little personal space as we raced from campus to campus, refueling constantly on caffeine and chocolate milkshakes in order to keep up with our tight meeting schedules.

At one point we had to split up in order to visit multiple campuses at the same time. It was during this stretch that my colleague narrowly avoided a serious accident while driving in bad weather on a highway. Badly shaken up by this incident, she drove to the nearest commercial airport, dropped off the rental car and bought a one-way ticket home so that she could rest and recover.

On my own now, I only managed to keep going a week longer before I ran completely out of steam and had a breakdown. I was a nervous wreck and spent hours hiding from public view and trying to get a grip on my emotions. Waves of anxiety would wash over me unexpectedly, and I was plagued by vivid nightmares that kept me up at night and made me afraid to fall back asleep. My appetite disappeared, and when I did eat I often experienced irritable bowel syndrome. I was a mess.

One of my best friends and housemates was able to take some time off of work and fly out to meet me on the road. He accompanied me to a final campus visit on the East Coast, and then I suspended the tour, and we drove back to Chicago so I could begin the slow journey toward recovery.

THE ROAD TO RENEWAL

One of the scariest parts of burning out is the despairing feeling of being out of control. This was a new experience for me, and for whatever reason evenings tended to be the hardest part of each day. It wasn't a simple matter of getting a couple nights of good sleep and then bouncing back to normal. I had been pushing myself too far for too long and it was going to take a while to recover my emotional and physical health. If we don't stop on our own, eventually our bodies stop for us. And this is true no matter what form workaholism may take in each of us—whether it's long hours at the office, conducting case visits all days of the week, working on emails through the night and so forth.

During this trying season a number of older and wiser friends came around me in support and prayer. Together, we explored the ways that I had gotten off track and developed a personal renewal plan to help me regain a more healthy and balanced life. It was reassuring to have a roadmap, but it would still take a couple more months before I felt mostly healed.

In the meantime, the renewal plan became a long-overdue opportunity to intentionally think through how I should order my days so that I—and my activism—could remain more faithfully and sustainably grounded in Christ. In addition to practical work boundaries and lifestyle habits (including improved diet and exercise), the plan addressed three key areas or disciplines that are easy but costly to neglect in our social action: sabbath, contemplation and community.

Each of these biblical disciplines is an integral part of Christian discipleship, and they're especially critical when it comes to our social action. Neglecting all three to varying extents is what ultimately led to my burnout.

I already knew the importance of contemplation and community, but the busier things became the less time I found to spend in prayer and reflection. And the more I traveled, the harder it was to stay connected to any stable community. This needed to change, and I'll explore these two disciplines further in chapters thirteen and fourteen respectively.

When it came to the sabbath, however, I was starting from scratch. I had never practiced taking a regular sabbath. This would have seemed absurd to generations of faithful Jews and Christians, but sadly is all too common among many of us today.

REMEMBERING THE SABBATH

Are any of the Ten Commandments optional?[1]

Most, if not all of us, would say absolutely not! We're still not supposed to lie, steal, covet, murder or commit adultery. We *are* called to honor our parents and respect God's name. And we're certainly not to worship any idols or follow other gods.

Yet, even as political battles are waged over where and how the Ten Commandments can be displayed in public, many of us are breaking the fourth commandment regularly and without thinking twice. "Remember the Sabbath day by keeping it holy," it begins. It's not a suggestion; it's a directive. As Matthew Sleeth, author of the book *24/6*, is fond of saying, this is the longest of the commandments and the only one that begins with the word *remember*, as if God knew we would forget. The fourth commandment continues:

> Six days you shall labor and do all your work, but the seventh day is a sabbath to the LORD your God. On it you shall not do any work, neither you, nor your son or daughter, nor your male or

female servant, nor your animals, nor any foreigner residing in your towns. For in six days the LORD made the heavens and the earth, the sea, and all that is in them, but he rested on the seventh day. Therefore the LORD blessed the Sabbath day and made it holy. (Exodus 20:8-11)

The sabbath is a gift from God that provides for good and healthy living, no matter what our specific calling may be. It's a rich and powerful principle that runs deep throughout the Scriptures and extends to every living thing. Even the land itself has sabbath rights.

In Leviticus, God warns the Israelites that if they do not live faithfully before him, which includes observing the sabbath and allowing their servants, livestock and even the land to enjoy the sabbath as well, then he will send them into exile. "Then the land will rest and enjoy its sabbaths years," Leviticus 26:34-35 reads. "All the time that it lies desolate, the land will have the rest it did not have during the sabbaths you lived in it." This warning came to pass generations later when the Israelites were conquered and sent into exile: "He carried into exile to Babylon the remnant, who escaped from the sword. . . . The land enjoyed its sabbath rests; all the time of its desolation it rested, until the seventy years were completed in fulfillment of the word of the LORD spoken by Jeremiah" (2 Chronicles 36:20-21).

There were many reasons why the Jews ended up going into exile, but violating the sabbath was notably one of them. Perhaps it's time for us to take this discipline more seriously today.

And why wouldn't we?

More than a mandate, the sabbath is a gift from God that helps us remain centered. It reminds us that we are human *beings*, not human *doings*, and that we are created to *be* in right relationship with God, each other and all of creation.

The sabbath helps us focus on God. By pausing from our striving, we acknowledge that God is sovereign and the fate of the world doesn't ultimately rest on our efforts. We surrender ourselves to God and trust in his timing and provision. As Bethany Hoang puts it in *Deepening the Soul for Justice*, "The resting and stopping of sabbath are intended as being good in and of themselves—complete. They are a declaration of all that has come before as belonging to God, and a declaration that all that is left undone and all that lies ahead also belongs to God. All is from God and for God and by God."[2]

In a very tangible way, practicing the sabbath shows and grows our faith in a God who is in control and whose kingdom advances with our meaningful participation, but is in no way dependent on us in order to succeed. This discipline helps us to keep Christ at the center of our lives and our social action, and works against the temptation to idolize ourselves, others or the cause (see chap. 10).

The sabbath is also a time of remembrance and gratitude. If things are going well, we remember that Jesus is the vine and we are branches; without him we can do nothing (John 15:5). If things are going poorly, we remember that in the midst of trouble we can take heart and find peace in Christ, for he has overcome the world (John 16:33).

At a very practical level the sabbath is also about us. God created humans to work as well as to rest; to be active as well as to stop. Stopping is critical to our long-term health and well-being, as I learned during my burnout period. We regularly need renewal, and the sabbath provides us with just such an opportunity. It prioritizes faithfulness over effectiveness and is a prophetic discipline in a world that idolizes productivity.

Learning to Stop

The law of inertia states that an object at rest stays at rest and an object in motion stays in motion. Unless, that is, a force of some sort is applied to stop it or change its direction. The same is true of our lives and our social action. There is great inertia in the status quo. We're constantly in motion, and it will take an intentional effort to slow down and stop. In other words, the sabbath is something we need to learn how to practice.

Stopping can be hard for many of us. It can seem like we're being lazy or underproductive when there's so much that always needs to be done. I often struggle with feeling insecure about falling behind in my work compared to those who don't take a sabbath. The sabbath has almost always been countercultural in society, although these days it's also countercultural throughout much of the church. This means we'll always readily have reasons why we can't afford to stop.

Early into my congressional run, I ended up having a heated argument with my first campaign manager over whether I would continue to take a weekly sabbath, which included going to church on Sunday. Typically, this would be unthinkable in a political campaign—there's just never enough time to spare. Yet I knew from painful personal experience that this was a commitment I couldn't compromise on. Taking a sabbath almost every week throughout the campaign was one way that I could honor God and help keep from burning out again.

Successfully observing the sabbath requires planning and determination: planning in order to set aside time and take care of the things we need to get out of the way (including personal errands and chores), and determination in order to guard the time and keep any and all distractions from encroaching.

Of course, the sabbath doesn't have to take place on Saturday, Sunday or any other particular day of the week. Although many people find that it helps to be relatively consistent if possible. And it doesn't need to be limited to one day a week either. Shorter rests can (and probably should) be incorporated more often, and longer sabbaticals are worth building in when possible, especially in between major life and job transitions.

Without being too prescriptive—there are many ways to observe the sabbath—what we actually do can vary, as long as it's God-centering and restful. Being an introvert, it's life-giving for me to spend more time alone or with a few close friends during sabbaths. In addition to going to church (if on a Sunday) and investing more time in quiet prayer, I often use the day to go for casual hikes in a nearby forest preserve, read books that build up my faith, take afternoon naps as needed, go for a run to stretch myself out or otherwise do things that help renew my body and spirit. This also means fasting from work, chores and often even the Internet.

Putting physical distance in between us and our work can be very valuable as well. For this reason, many of my friends involved in community development and other place-based ministries often spend days off away from their neighborhoods or churches. I also talk to a lot of college students who go off campus to nearby coffee shops, bookstores or forest preserves so that they get a change of scenery.

Taking Longer Breaks

Stopping regularly helps us to persevere in doing good over the long haul. But there are also times when we may be so burned-out that we will need not just a weekly sabbath but also a longer sabbatical.

In some cases, as with many professors and pastors, we may qualify for a regular sabbatical through our church or organization. A lot of us probably don't have this option available, however, and there can come a point when we might even need to resign from our job or ministry in order to take a season off to do something completely different. This could include going back to school, staying at home to look after family members, writing a book or even finding another field of work. After all, what's the point of gaining the whole world if we lose our souls in the process (Matthew 16:26; Mark 8:36; Luke 9:25)? It's much better to stop first.

After my congressional campaign ended, for example, I was blessed to be able to head down to South Florida to stay with my grandmother and spend a few months recovering on the beach or in a fishing kayak. After this extended period of rest I found myself ready and eager to jump back into social action. It was at this time that God provided me with a job offer from the Evangelical Environmental Network, which I gladly accepted.

AN ONGOING JOURNEY

Pursuing social justice is often overwhelming and discouraging. It's a sobering realization that many of us either have faced or will face what is often called "soul fatigue" or what I've described in this chapter as "burnout." God worked through my painful burnout experience to recenter and prepare me for the tougher challenges ahead, and a big part of the process was remembering the sabbath and striving to keep it holy.

One final point I'd like to make is that there's a temptation not only to forget or ignore the sabbath but also to become too legalistic about keeping it. In the Gospels, the Pharisees challenged Jesus for violating their interpretation of the sabbath by letting his disciples glean for food and by performing a miracle that they considered to be work. However, Jesus saw through their legal traps, just as he sees through any of ours today. He responded to the Pharisees by asserting his authority as Lord of the sabbath and challenging them to consider whether it is ultimately lawful on the sabbath to do good or to do evil (Matthew 12:1-14; Mark 3:1-6; Luke 6:1-10). As Matthew Sleeth puts it, "It may be against the law to harvest grain on the Sabbath, but it is never wrong to feed the hungry. The laws against working were made to benefit people, not the other way around."[3]

That said, and to be completely transparent, I'm still growing a lot in this area. At times I still have to travel or work on a Sunday but fail to set aside another day of rest in its place. On other occasions I get drawn into unforeseen or poorly planned personal commitments that leave me harried and overcommitted during what was supposed to be a day of rest. And even when things go exactly as planned I'm ever conscious of how much I yet have to learn about truly resting before God. Can you relate to struggles like these?

There are many problems in the world. And the sabbath won't fix them all. But it does help put our lives into proper perspective. It honors God and renews us for the ongoing journey. And it is a powerful testimony of our faith in a God who is ultimately in control and who invites us to worship and follow him in freedom and peace.

FOR REFLECTION AND APPLICATION

1. Do you have anyone in your life who's asking you questions such as, *Are you getting enough rest? Are you overworked? Do you have a sabbath? Are you burning out?* If so, who? If not, who might do this for you?

2. Describe your own weekly sabbath. How is it different from your other days? How is it the same?

3. Is it hard for you to take a sabbath each week? What are some of the internal and external pressures and expectations that make you reluctant to take your foot off the gas pedal of your work?

4. When we take no breaks and have no sabbaths, is it only ourselves we are hurting? If you have workaholic tendencies, think about the ways your workaholism needs to be supported by those you rely on. How has your own refusal to rest caused stress for other people?

5. Reflect on this verse and ask for the Lord's help to live it:

   Be still and know that I am God;
   > I will be exalted among the nations,
   > I will be exalted in the earth. (Psalm 46:10)

13

CONTEMPLATION

Jesus often withdrew to lonely places and prayed.

LUKE 5:16

"SEEKING JUSTICE DOESN'T BEGIN AT THE DOOR OF A BROTHEL," writes Bethany Hoang. "Seeking justice begins with seeking the God of justice."[1]

Many of us struggle to balance action with contemplation. But our calling is not just about doing things *for* God; it's first and foremost about being *with* God. How can contemplation help ground our social action and our identity in an intimate relationship with the one who is our Creator, Sustainer and Redeemer?

I'll always remember my first visit to International Justice Ministry's office in Washington, DC. I was there to learn about their work on college campuses and explore ways to collaborate together. But when 11 a.m. came, the person I was meeting with asked if we could pause our discussion for their daily office-wide prayer meeting. *Your daily what?* I thought to myself in surprise.

I've always had great respect for IJM's mission and ministry. But I didn't realize how intentionally they've integrated contemplation as a priority throughout their work. It's the first thing that happens every morning, Hoang shares, as each staff person arrives at the office and switches off their phone and email.

> For the first thirty minutes of every day, we make a declaration to ourselves and to God that the first work of seeking justice is the work of prayer. It is the work of being still before the God who knows more of the reality of injustice than we will ever know, the God who alone can move and act through us to bring about greater levels of transformation than we could ever even begin to dream of on our own.[2]

Then, as I experienced during my visit, the staff at every IJM office around the world come together at an agreed upon time every day to reflect on a psalm and pray for each other and the cases that they're working on. In addition to these daily gatherings, they also set aside four full days every year for corporate contemplation and a fifth day solely for personal solitude.

Why set aside all this time for contemplation when there's so much justice to actively fight for?

IJM has a remarkable track record of making a tangible difference for victims of injustice, particularly those trapped in modern-day slavery. A key part of what centers and sustains their fruitful ministry, however, is that they grasp and practice the counterintuitive truth that faithful social action and contemplation always go hand in hand.

Mary Versus Martha

I'm action-oriented when it comes to work and ministry. Unless I'm intentionally in vacation or sabbath mode, if I'm not getting something done then it's easy to feel like I'm just wasting valuable time. This reaction is a common struggle among those of us who are geared more toward action. As Richard Lovelace writes, "Most of those who are praying are not praying about social issues and most of those who are active in social issues are not praying very much."[3]

In the Gospel account, when Jesus visited Mary and Martha's home,

Mary sat at Christ's feet and listened to him talk while her sister, Martha, ran around getting everything ready. "Lord, don't you care that my sister has left me to do the work by myself?" Martha complained. "Tell her to help me!" But Jesus replied, "Martha, Martha, you are worried and upset about many things, but few things are needed—or indeed only one. Mary has chosen what is better, and it will not be taken away from her" (Luke 10:38-42).

Who do you relate to more in this story—Mary or Martha? Granted, this is a somewhat false dichotomy, as none of us are fully one or the other. That said, however, I've always wanted to be like Mary, but the reality is that I've always related to and sympathized more with Martha. Activism comes naturally to me in many ways, while contemplation is a far more tedious discipline, which makes writing this chapter particularly challenging. But contemplation is still critical, even (and especially) for those of us who struggle with it. We're called to engage in social action out of our love relationship with God, not just because we care about a particular cause. This means that our social action flows out of our contemplation, and that our contemplation likewise flows out of our social action.

In Luke 4:31-44, Jesus is teaching at the synagogue and astonishes everyone by casting out a demon from a man. News about him spreads like wildfire across the surrounding area. Jesus then heads over to Simon's home where he cures Simon's mother-in-law of a high fever. As evening approaches, crowds of people flock to the house hoping that Jesus will heal their sick and demon possessed. His success and popularity is soaring. What does Jesus do next? He goes off to a solitary place and, based on what we know from other parts of the Gospels, he withdraws in order to pray. When Jesus comes back he tells the crowds that it's time for him to move on to another place, leaving the massively "successful" work at hand. Why? Because Jesus understood, as we do well to remember today, that his work wasn't about worldly measures of "success" but about obediently carrying out the will of his heavenly Father.

So how can contemplation fit into and strengthen our pursuit of justice and compassion today? Building on the ground covered in chapter twelve about practicing the sabbath, the rest of this chapter will focus on four ways that our contemplation and social action belong together.

CONTEMPLATION KEEPS US CENTERED

The first way that contemplation is indispensible to our social action is that it keeps us centered on Christ. Bethany Hoang writes,

> When we spread out our discouragements before the Lord—the lies waged against the reality of God's reign, the taunts hurled against our belief in God's power to intervene and to heal and to redeem—this simple act of choosing to come before the Lord and seek his face is an act of proclaiming the truth that God is the good, the just, the sovereign Ruler of the ages over and against the brutality of the moment.[4]

By turning our gaze to Jesus instead of fixating on the problems of the world, we can better keep from becoming weary, bitter and cynical. It's easy to lose sight of God and become immersed in and overwhelmed by the unjust situations and people we're up against. To quote a line often attributed to Oswald Chambers, "We have to pray with our eyes on God, not on the difficulties."

Likewise, if we become visibly successful, the resulting praise and popularity can easily go straight to our pride. Such attention is seductive, and it's very hard to keep our egos from overinflating unless we continually humble ourselves before God. We can learn from Jesus here, who, in spite of being in constantly high demand, regularly withdrew from the crowds to commune with his heavenly Father. In the same way, fixing our eyes on God instead of on ourselves, will help to keep us grounded in kingdom reality.

The woods of northern Michigan are one of my favorite places to be during the summer. I often stay at the Au Sable Institute, which sits on a beautiful forested campus that includes a groundwater-fed wetland called Louis' Pond.

The largely refugee and immigrant neighborhood I live in outside of Chicago is always noisy and bustling with social activity. In contrast, Au Sable is equally alive but in a much more serene and secluded way. I love wandering along the winding wooded trails, breathing in the warm scent of baking pine needles, while listening to the tall trunks creak gently from side to side, their leaves rustling in the breeze and scattering rays of sunlight across the colorful forest floor.

At night I love to sit on the dock overlooking Louis' Pond, alternately mesmerized by the dancing glow of fireflies below and the brilliant glimmering of the Milky Way above. I do a lot of praying on this dock—contemplation comes more naturally here. Some people have no trouble quieting their hearts in the middle of a congested urban scene, and that's great. But for me Louis' Pond is the perfect place to slow down and soak in the beauty of God's world.

And I'm not alone in this experience. Many others also find that it's easier to feel close to God at a place like Au Sable. I've retreated to this spot in the midst of some of the busiest times of my life, such as during the congressional campaign, when I've started a new job and during major writing projects. I always enter feeling like a muddled mess. Slowly but surely, however, my spirit is renewed as I commune with God under the stars, reflecting on his majesty, remembering his unfailing love and recentering on my secure identity as his beloved child.

Contemplation Helps Us Process

The second way contemplation fits in with social action is that it helps us to process the things that are happening in and around us. This is not only healthy but can lead to wiser and more balanced decisions.

Consider the story of Moses killing an Egyptian he saw mistreating a Hebrew (Exodus 2:11-15). He witnessed an injustice and acted immediately. Perhaps even compulsively. His reaction was rash and violent and resulted not only in a dead body but also in Moses losing credibility with his fellow Hebrews and having to flee into the desert. Without jumping to conclusions about Moses' walk with God back then, I think it's fair to say that contemplation can help ground us in God's wisdom so that we react better when challenges and crises arise.

Pursuing social justice can be a long and hard road, often filled with a rollercoaster of highs and lows. Plans can get confusing, relationships can grow complicated and outcomes can be elusive. Stress builds and tensions grow. It's easy to drown ourselves in busyness, using our efforts to change the world as a distraction from confronting what needs to change in our own lives. As Socrates pointed out, however, "the unexamined life is not worth living."

It's important to regularly reflect on our days, our activism and ourselves. Spiritual formation directors and writers refer to this as the "daily examen" and the prayer of examen—spiritual disciplines in which we examine and process our daily events. Such times of contemplation create the space for us to hear from the Holy Spirit, whether it's about the ways God wants to convict or heal us or the ways he wants to direct our service and witness. As we reflect we not only become more aware of our internal and external realities, but we can also come to recognize God's presence and leading amidst our circumstances.

Too often we let our mission become defined or derailed by public opinion and demand. This is a common challenge in social action generally, but I especially struggled with it a lot during my congressional campaign. As I shared in chapter two, I entered the race with a strong sense of calling and a vision to lift up the voices and struggles of people on the margins. Being a candidate, however, I found myself constantly being pulled in all sorts of directions by the advisers, donors and voters around me. I knew the main issues I felt called to focus on—immigration reform, environmental stewardship and the corrupting influence of money in politics—but it sure was hard to stay on track from day to day. While I didn't spend as much time in contemplation as I wanted to during the hectic campaign, the times I did helped me to process the feedback I was constantly receiving without losing focus on God's calling.

Even as the crowds clamored around Jesus, as we saw in Luke 4, he showed compassion for them without being diverted from where God was leading him next. By seeking solitude in the midst of his busy ministry, Jesus was able to maintain a clear vision of God's will, even though it took him into new territory. Practicing contemplation as Jesus did gives us an opportunity to intentionally process life with God and remain receptive to the Spirit's leading.

Contemplation Gives Us Strength

The third reason contemplation is so critical to our social action is that it gives us the strength to keep going.

Some people—by the sheer force of their personality—are able to endure intense, long-term activism without burning out. But regardless of how tough we are, or how long we think we can last on our own, we shouldn't fool ourselves. At the end of the day we're all finite and fallen humans without the capacity to save ourselves, let alone this broken world; we all need to rely on God to sustain us.

The night that Jesus was betrayed he took his disciples into the Garden of Gethsemane and prayed to his Father for help. He knew the horror and suffering that was to come and was overcome with anguish. The Father heard his prayer and answered, not by sparing his Son from the cross but by sending an angel from heaven to strengthen him (Luke 22:41-43).

In the same way, when Jesus calls us to take up our crosses daily and follow him, he doesn't promise that we will be spared hardship. On the contrary, he tells us to expect it. But God does promise that those who depend on him will renew their strength,

They will soar on wings like eagles;
    they will run and not grow weary,
    they will walk and not be faint. (Isaiah 40:31)

As we learn from Jesus, the greater the adversity, whether in our social action or any other facet of our lives, the faster we should be driven to our knees as we seek God's strength to persevere.

A friend named Darryl moved into a diverse low-income neighborhood far rougher than the one I live in. Though I'm part of an established Christian intentional community, he and his one roommate were alone in their efforts. They went in with a heart to serve the community but without any training or experienced mentors. As they juggled part-time jobs and full-time course loads, they attempted to run a small afterschool children's program, build relationships with their neighbors and help address the many needs in the community.

Darryl dealt with more crises that one year than he had experienced in his entire life until then. Some of the kids in their program lost family members to prison. Theft and prostitution were common. And from time to time drunken brawls would spill into the courtyard. A handicapped woman who lived directly below them with her two mentally ill children died violently late one night, and Darryl and his roommate found her body and called the police. Whether wisely or not, they even ended up housing an antagonistic homeless man in their apartment for almost a month before things finally boiled over and Darryl burned out.

Recalling this trying period, Darryl tells me that through it all, he continually found strength while seeking God in prayer, both in solitude and with his roommate. He would wake up early every morning and spend an hour or more praying and meditating on Scripture. Amid the pain and drama going on all around him, these regular times of contemplation helped give him the endurance to persevere and slowly but surely recover.

CONTEMPLATION AS ACTION

Finally, contemplation is, in and of itself, a form of action.

When we see injustice, our first instinct may be to go do something practical about it. Which usually doesn't mean praying. Yet prayer is one of the most practical and effective things we can do, and it's always available to us. "Ask and it will be given to you; seek and you will find; knock and the door will be opened to you. For everyone who asks receives; the one who seeks finds; and to the one who knocks, the door will be opened" (Matthew 7:7-8). God hears and answers our prayers, sometimes by using us, and sometimes by moving others or intervening directly in miraculous ways.

Darryl was always looking for people willing to visit his neighborhood and help out in the afterschool program he was running. In particular, however, he was looking for the right person to take it over once he and his roommate graduated from college and likely moved out of town. Darryl attended a major state university that is also one of the biggest party schools in the nation. One day, as he was on a prayer walk around his campus in between classes, he sat down next to another student on a bench. He had never met this young woman before but sensed a distinct nudge from the Holy Spirit to speak to her. As they began to chat, he learned that Sarah was a fellow Christian who was looking for a ministry to get involved in. Recognizing the opportunity, he invited her to be part of the afterschool program in his neighborhood, and Sarah jumped right in.

A year later Darryl and his roommate graduated and moved on to graduate school elsewhere. The afterschool program went through a period of ups and downs and even got to the point where it disbanded for a season. Through it all, Sarah remained a constant thread that held the program together. Even when everyone else drifted away, she continued to show up each week in order to be with the kids. Because of Sarah's faithfulness, the program was eventually reborn and is thriving today. And it may never have happened if Darryl hadn't been prayerfully listening for the leading of the Holy Spirit.

When we pray, God works.

PRACTICING THE PRESENCE

What does contemplation look like as we pursue social justice?

In *Doing Evangelism Jesus' Way,* Ron Sider gives numerous examples of social reformers who grounded their action in prayer.

William Wilberforce and the other members of the Clapham Sect were the leaders in the British crusade to abolish the slave trade. Historians tell us that they immersed their political strategizing and lobbying in daily three-hour sessions of intercessory prayer. Later in the nineteenth century Lord Shaftesbury spearheaded a large number of social reforms, ending child labor and reforming the factories. When his son asked how he could do so many things at once, he replied, "By hearty prayer to Almighty God before I begin, by entering into it with faith and zeal, and by making my end to be His glory and the good of mankind." Charles Finney was the Billy Graham of the nineteenth century, and he was also a leading crusader against slavery. He insisted that long hours of intercessory prayer were central to his work. Finney would have appreciated what Helmut Thielicke has said of Martin Luther: He prayed four hours each day, "not despite his busy life, but because only so could he accomplish his gigantic labors."[5]

Contemplation begins with grounding our social action in its biblical and theological foundation, and cultivating regular space and time to meditate on Scripture and seek the Lord in prayer. This takes place in both solitude and community, and can involve set liturgies as well as unstructured times of prayer and silence. The specifics will vary as we each spend time communing with God in ways that fit how he has wired us.

I recently talked with a fellow author and spiritual director who pointed out that things like running and fishing can often be part of our solitude and contemplation. Such activities keep our bodies engaged while freeing up our minds to pray and process with fewer distractions. Which is all the reason I need to go fishing more often!

Jo Anne Lyon is the general superintendent of the Wesleyan Church, which is a major evangelical denomination with around five thousand churches and mission efforts in eighty countries. She's also been a lifelong activist on numerous justice issues and previously founded a relief and development agency called World Hope. I can't imagine how busy she must be. I once asked Rev. Lyon how she has found the strength to handle such demanding responsibilities for so many years. Her answer was simple: she makes it a priority to balance her action with contemplation, striving to set aside an hour every day, a day every week and a week every year to be still before God. If someone with her schedule and responsibilities can make this work, then certainly someone like me should be able to as well!

However we pursue contemplation, it belongs as an integral part of our social action as we continually strive to make God the center of our lives. As the seventeenth-century Parisian monastic Brother Lawrence once prayed, "O my God, since thou art with me, and I must now, in obedience to thy commands, apply my mind to these outward things, I beseech thee to grant me the grace to continue in thy presence; and to this end do thou prosper me with thy assistance, receive all my works, and possess all my affections."[6]

FOR REFLECTION AND APPLICATION

1. According to Richard Lovelace, "Most of those who are praying are not praying about social issues and most of those who are active in social issues are not praying very much." To what extent is that true of you, your colaborers in social action and your church?

2. "We have to pray with our eyes on God, not on the difficulties," says Oswald Chambers. It may be necessary to periodically withdraw to lonely or solitary places in order to do that. Do you have a place where you can retreat to do this? Explain.

3. When things are going well and you're busy doing good and are being applauded and validated in your work, do you ever pause to "intentionally process life with God and remain receptive to the

Spirit's leading"? If so, what is the secret to doing this? If not, why?

4. As you engage in activism, what should a contemplative life look like for you?

5. In the Gospels we see an active Jesus, much in demand and doing much good, yet leading a contemplative life. Pray that your life may also become Christlike in this sense: "But Jesus often withdrew to lonely places and prayed" (Luke 5:16).

14

COMMUNITY

Now you are the body of Christ,
and each one of you is a part of it.

1 CORINTHIANS 12:27

IT'S EASY TO BECOME UPROOTED AND ISOLATED when working on justice issues, especially on national or global scales. In order to be healthy and sustainable, however, our social action needs to be both a collective effort as well as grounded in a community and place. How can we intentionally cultivate community as we pursue justice locally and beyond?

Lessons from Malawi

It was a two-day flight from my home in Chicago to Lilongwe, the capital of Malawi, which included a cramped overnight layover in Nairobi, Kenya. But it was worth it. Our friends at Tearfund UK and the Malawi Eagles, a national evangelical relief and development organization, had invited us to bring a group of key leaders from the American church to witness the effects climate change is having on their country. Our team included Jenny Yang from World Relief,

Jonathan Merritt from Religion News Service, former US diplomat Judd Birdsall, Karen Swallow Prior from Liberty University, Leroy Barber from Mission Year (now at Word Made Flesh), writer and speaker Margot Starbuck, and Noel Castellanos from the Christian Community Development Association.

There's still a lot of confusion and controversy in the American church around how the climate is changing and whether it's a problem. But there's little doubt in the rest of the world. Millions of people are already suffering from the effects of climate disruption, which continue to intensify, especially among the poor and vulnerable. During our visit we met with a respected Malawian development expert who warned us that climate change has become a greater crisis in his country than even HIV/AIDS.

This isn't something we usually hear in our churches in the United States. We're still insulated enough from our surroundings to question the changing climate patterns that others are experiencing as a destabilizing reality. So over the course of an eye-opening week, the Malawi Eagles staff took us to visit some of the communities they've been working in for years so we could see and hear what's going on firsthand. We were there to learn about both the bad news of climate impacts, as well as the good news of how communities and churches are working together to respond and adapt.

Every morning our team would pile into Land Rovers and journey down into the Rift Valley, crossing the mighty Shire River and bumping along a series of unmarked dirt roads until we somehow managed to arrive at the right destination. Waiting to greet us would be a group of village leaders led by the local chief. After a welcome song and dance, we'd gather around in a circle for introductions and a discussion on what that particular village was dealing with. We'd then break up into smaller groups and visit individual families to talk further and pray together. They prayed that we would have success in mobilizing our churches around climate action, while we prayed that they would have enough food and income for the year ahead.

Our team learned a lot from these villages, and we returned to the United States brimming with ideas and inspiration, eagerly reengaging our churches and networks around the moral urgency to act on climate change. In particular, though, one of the greatest lessons I took away from that visit was how critical and powerful community can be in our efforts to overcome injustice and help make the world better.

The resilient people of Malawi are facing overwhelming challenges: poverty, HIV/AIDS, malaria, unsafe water, and now worsening droughts, floods and failing crops. Climate change is undoing a lot of the development progress they've made over recent decades and is straining their ability to grow enough food for their families to survive.

But with the help of national church-based organizations like the Malawi Eagles, villages are organizing themselves and coming together to pursue creative collective solutions that are strengthening their individual families as well as their overall communities. They're building and maintaining levies to hold back the flash floods that result from increasingly common but unpredictable downpours. They're forming community-based savings and loan groups that foster healthy saving habits while providing sustainable loans to each other for investments that can improve their long-term well-being and security. They're implementing conservation agriculture techniques to increase yields while protecting the land. They're replanting forests, investing in solar power, starting up childcare programs to free up working adults, and so on.

I distinctly remember talking to one mother who was part of a savings and loan group. "Life was much harder before we started this group," she shared, "but now I've been able to borrow money to build a home for my family. I paid back the loan on time and have also started saving money to send my children to secondary school. I have so much more hope for our future now."

The problems are still daunting, and their future is still far from secure. But by working together in community, villages have been able to make very real improvements in their food security and financial stability. On their own, many families would stand little chance of survival. Together, however, they're finding ways to scrape by, strengthen one another and push forward.

SEEKING JUSTICE TOGETHER

Faithful social action is grounded in community.

Being a Christian means being a part of the family of God. It has become trendy to disparage the church and withdraw to pursue Christ individually. Or to try and be "spiritual but not religious" Christians. But following Jesus doesn't work like that. We may not like the church—and there are good reasons to be unhappy—but as Eugene Peterson put it: "We are a family in Christ. When we become Christians, we are among brothers and sisters in faith. No Christian is an only child."[1]

The apostle Paul describes us as together forming a body—the body of Christ:

> Just as a body, though one, has many parts, but all its many parts form one body, so it is with Christ. For we were all baptized by one Spirit so as to form one body—whether Jews or Gentiles, slave or free—and we were all given the one Spirit to drink. Even so the body is not made up of one part but of many.
>
> Now if the foot should say, "Because I am not a hand, I do not belong to the body," it would not for that reason stop being part of the body. And if the ear should say, "Because I am not an eye, I do not belong to the body," it would not for that reason stop being part of the body. If the whole body were an eye, where would the sense of hearing be? If the whole body were an ear, where would the sense of smell be? But in fact God has placed the parts in the body, every one of them, just as he wanted them to be. If they were all one part, where would the body be? As it is, there are many parts, but one body. (1 Corinthians 12:12-20)

He goes on to talk about how each part of the body has value and is indispensible, driving his analogy home by concluding that "you are the body of Christ, and each one of you is a part of it" (1 Corinthians 12:27). This holds just as true for our social action as it does for the rest of our lives. Some of us are communicators, some are prophets, some are social workers, some are philanthropists, some are managers, some are pastors, some are organizers, some are board members, some are issue or policy experts. We're each part of the body, and we each have our God-given gifts to contribute and roles to play.

We are created for and called to community. Can you think of anyone who would rather face injustice on his or her own? We may not always like the particular company we have, but that doesn't mean we don't want community; it just means we want better or more suitable company. It's true that some of us are more independent by temperament, at least when things are going well, but when trials and challenges loom we often remember the value of being more interdependent.

In different ways and at varying levels we all long for people who understand and care about us, who share our burdens and celebrate our joys, and who will stand with us even when things get hard or we get messy. We all long to belong.

ISLANDS AND NOMADS

This deep-seated human desire for belonging exists in constant tension with our highly mobile and individualistic culture. While the Bible comes out of a traditional collectivistic culture, we in the United States are part of one of the most individualistic society in the world today.

Healthy communities are able to strike a complementary balance between freedom and responsibility. It's about more than the right to exercise our freedom as long as it doesn't impinge on the rights of others. It's also about the responsibility to value the common good. Obviously we tend to be better at the former than the latter.

In American culture the interest of each individual typically trumps the interest of the collective, whether that's a family, church, organization or any other level of community. In this way we enjoy the benefits of community but shirk the responsibilities. We try to act like we're islands unto ourselves, except of course when and where we want help.

We also live in a society that has become remarkably uprooted and transitory. It used to be that communities were more stable and families tended to live around one another. Apart from fighting in wars, it was less common for people to leave home for long periods of time or to move around every few years. Today, however, that exception has become the norm. Many of us are now functional nomads. It's normal to cross the country for college or change jobs every few years. That's just a part of life, though one of the consequences is that we lack a deep sense of place or much long-term community. When we become isolated like this we're especially vulnerable to temptation, bitterness and soul fatigue.

This individualistic and transient mentality easily overflows into our social action as well. Leading up to my burnout (see chap. 12), I was constantly on the road, going from campus to campus, church to church and conference to conference. I had good friends to live with, a local church that I was integrated into and many potential advisers and mentors. But they were all back home, and I often wasn't. I cared deeply about community, but until I hit burnout I wasn't taking it seriously enough.

WHY WE NEED COMMUNITY

There are a number of good reasons to take community seriously in our social action. I'll briefly discuss three of them.

First, community gives us resilience. We need each other in order to keep up the good fight for justice. As King Solomon advised:

Two are better than one,
    because they have a good return for their labor:
If either of them falls down,
    one can help the other up.

But pity anyone who falls
   and has no one to help them up.
Also, if two lie down together, they will keep warm.
   But how can one keep warm alone?
Though one may be overpowered,
   two can defend themselves.
A cord of three strands is not quickly broken. (Ecclesiastes 4:9-12)

There is strength in numbers, and when it comes to community, the whole is truly greater than the sum of its parts. There are many needs and challenges in life that we can't tackle on our own—communities can accomplish things that individuals can't.

Our team saw this clearly demonstrated while in Malawi. By pooling together their talents, time and resources, villages were making remarkable progress under very trying circumstances. Going back to the apostle Paul's analogy of the church being a body, we all have different personal strengths and weaknesses; we need all of our parts to work together for the body to function in a healthy and effective way.

Second, community gives us support. Being disconnected and isolated in our social action leaves us much more susceptible to loneliness, depression, anger, bitterness, temptation and corruption. Safe and vulnerable community offers us the gifts of accountability and encouragement. This only gets more critical over the long haul when the going gets tough and our defenses grow weak.

We all know too many tragic examples of prominent Christian leaders who succumbed to some form of illicit or immoral behavior. Often, these incidents could have been prevented or at least addressed earlier if the leaders in question were more deeply plugged into community and had more rigorous accountability. It's not just leaders who struggle, but their failures cause a bigger stir given their prominence and responsibilities. Wouldn't it be good to learn this lesson without having to fall into the trap ourselves?

On a lighter note, community also provides us with fellowship and companionship. It doesn't just make our social action stronger; it also makes it a lot more fun. As we follow God's calling, it's life giving to enjoy solidarity with others in our shared mission, vision and circumstances. And it's a blessing to know that, whatever happens, there are people with whom we can weather disappointments and celebrate joys. Parties are always better with good friends and colleagues.

Third, community gives us roots. Being invested in a local community—both in terms of relationships and location—helps to ground our lives and our social action in a sense of place. Our heritage and our communities help make us who we are, and they provide much of the context through which we view and engage the world, and through which the world sees and engages us in return.

As such, social action is not just about how we address problems far away—especially for those like me who work on global issues for national organizations—it also needs to be how we help better the places God has planted us in. A wise social entrepreneur once advised me that social action is not merely about getting others to do things elsewhere. It also has to have tangible manifestations in our own neighborhoods and among our own people.

How We Cultivate Community

We experience community on many levels—as family, friends, churchgoers, neighbors, colleagues, classmates, roommates, mentors, prayer partners and, of course, as activists. As I wrote in chapter twelve, one of the first steps I took toward recovering from my burnout was to put together a personal renewal plan. Much of this plan reestablished healthy work and time boundaries; the rest reestablished healthy community.

Cultivating community takes time and intentionality, both of which are important for communicating value and demonstrating commitment.

Simply being present—and not constantly texting, tweeting or being otherwise absorbed in our smartphones—is the first step. (Though, of course, social media can be very helpful in sustaining relationships with family and friends who aren't in the same physical place.) So my plan started out by limiting how often and for how long I would travel. By setting boundaries around my travel, I could be home on a more regular basis, which in turn made it possible to reach out and invest more in my local church and neighborhood.

I've been actively involved in the same church now for more than a decade. I started attending while a freshman in college and was quickly plugged in as a youth group counselor and then missions committee member. While I remained in the same area after graduating, my work kept me on the road a lot, and this made it hard to stay connected and grounded at church. And I deeply missed the gift of worshiping regularly in a community I knew and who knew me. Since then, I've made it a priority to be back from most work trips in time to attend my own church on Sundays.

I've also made it a priority to invest more time and effort in sharing life with those around me. Traveling less means being more available and accessible, which is fundamental to being a good friend and neighbor. It means I can honor my commitment to my intentional community and stay abreast and involved in our neighborhood. This can include anything from chipping in when needs arise, such as when a baby is born or someone is moving, to simply opening up the apartment for folks to come hang out during evenings and weekends.

Being around more consistently also makes it easier to be intentional in finding common ground, building trust and growing in love. This is integral to fostering deep and lasting relationships.

At the most fundamental level we all have common ground with one another by virtue of our shared humanity. For Christians, however, Jesus is at the heart of our community. We may be particularly drawn to those who share our hobbies, vocations, political affiliations, food or entertainment preferences, or any number of other traits. But at the end of the day the most important thing we can have in common, and what binds us together even through our differences, is Jesus Christ.

Christian community is like a big bicycle wheel with Jesus at the hub and each of us at the end of a spoke on the outer rim. We're all connected to the hub and thus to each other, but as long as we're on the outer rim we remain far apart. As we make our way down each of our respective spokes, however, the closer we draw to the hub, which is Jesus, the closer we also get to one another.[2]

Trust is another critical aspect of strong and healthy community, though it's an endangered quality across much of society today. Surrounded by so much scandal, corruption, competition and manipulation, it's far easier to be cynical and suspicious than to be trusting and vulnerable. This may not be news when it comes to how we view politicians or the big banks, but what about the tragic sex-abuse scandals that continue to rock the church? Or what about the many ways that we often feel let down by those right around us? Our resulting environment of distrust is a major obstacle to building and sustaining healthy community at just about any level today. This puts us at a significant disadvantage when it comes to pursuing justice together.

So how can this change?

We cannot experience authentic community in the absence of trust, and this starts with us. Trust is something that we can intentionally build in ourselves and those around us. (An excellent book that covers this in detail is *The Speed of Trust* by Stephen M. R. Covey.) From the biblical perspective we're each called to be people who can be trusted; people who don't gossip (Proverbs 20:19), who keep our word (Matthew 5:33-37), who do honorable work (Colossians 3:23-24) and who sincerely look out for the welfare of others (Philippians 2:3-4).

Finally, cultivating community—and, for that matter, building trust—involves growing in love for one another (see chap. 6). As Shane Claiborne and Jonathan Wilson-Hartgrove paraphrase Dietrich Bonhoeffer, "The person who loves their dream of community will destroy community, but the person who loves those around them will create community."[3]

There's No Place Like Home

I'm blessed to live at Parkside (see chap. 8). Most of us who live here know each other and help look out for one another. I love returning

from work trips to hear my neighbors such as Wani, Guma and
Christian welcoming me home, and kids like Rashidi, Salama and Fisto
help carry my bags to the door (and then ask if they can come in and
play games). My neighbors are also why I've come to care so deeply
about issues such as welfare, affordable housing and immigration
reform. These aren't theoretical problems for me; they have faces,
names and stories, and they've befriended me. There's simply nowhere
else I'd rather live than here.

At the same time, however, living at Parkside can be hard and
wearisome. The level of need and injustice is often overwhelming and
discouraging, which is not unreasonable given the tragic circumstances
many of these families are coming from, and the completely foreign
situations they find themselves parachuted into here. There also
tends to be little privacy and few social boundaries, unless you invest
in thick curtains and keep your door locked (which is necessary at
times but also kind of defeats the whole purpose of being here).
Neighborhood kids often want to come over to play, and they have
no qualms peering through the cracks in the blinds and repeatedly
yelling my name if I don't answer the door. And then there's the
constant battle with the cockroaches and bedbugs.

In light of the challenges, what makes living here exponentially
better is the intentional Christian community I'm part of. In addition
to serving and learning from our neighbors, our group of twelve is also
intentional about cultivating community with one another. We meet
once a week at rotating apartments for dinner and gather for corporate prayer most evenings. We also spend time together beyond this,
sometimes just hanging out and other times working together on
neighborhood events (such as weekly Bible studies for the kids) or
other projects (such as the community garden).

To be transparent, living in intentional community is rarely as ro-
mantic or idealistic as it sounds. We see each other at our best, but we
also see each other at our worst. Personalities come into conflict, expectations clash, feelings are hurt and our weaknesses become glaring.

At the same time, it can be well worth it. Practicing such close Christian community brings to life Proverbs 27:17: "As iron sharpens iron, so one person sharpens another." It helps us to grow and keeps us accountable, and it provides great joy, solidarity and support, especially when things get tough and discouraging. As Psalm 133 put it so well:

> How good and pleasant it is
>   when God's people live together in unity!
> It is like precious oil poured on the head,
>   running down on the beard,
> running down on Aaron's beard,
>   down on the collar of his robe.
> It is as if the dew or Hermon
>   were falling on Mount Zion.
> For there the LORD bestows his blessing,
>   even life forevermore.

Of course, not everyone may find it feasible to live in an intentional community or in high-density apartments with lots of neighbors close by to build relationships with, or in rural farming communities that are more spread out but often still very connected. Nonetheless, we can all find opportunities to cultivate and invest in community wherever God places us—in our neighborhoods, workplaces, schools, churches and even in hospitals and prisons!

I think of the Norregaard family at my church, who open up their modest single-family home to hundreds of people every year. College students store boxes and furniture in their basement over the summer, church members hold small group meetings in their home every week, friends and friends of friends who need a place to stay are warmly welcomed—whether for a day or a month. They host so many guests that they've ended up replacing the regular lock on their front door with an electronic keypad. This way, instead of constantly duplicating keys they can now create unique codes for recurring visitors. The Norregaards live on a quiet street in a quiet suburb with fenced-in back yards. It would be easy to become isolated here—as many in similar contexts are. Yet by being intentional and hospitable, they've managed to foster a rich and vibrant community that blesses all those around them.

FOR REFLECTION AND APPLICATION

1. How long have you been a part of your current community? What do you do together—in terms of talents, time and resources—that makes it feel like a community?

2. What do you feel are the deficiencies of your community? Do you think those deficiencies are inherent in the community or derive from the extent of your investment in it?

3. If we want to deepen our involvement in community, we need to become trustworthy. Look up these passages to see what that involves: people who don't gossip (Proverbs 20:19), who keep our word (Matthew 5:33-37), who do honorable work (Colossians 3:23-24) and who sincerely look out for the welfare of others (Philippians 2:3-4).

4. Are there any practical steps you would like to take to deepen your involvement in community? What are they?

5. Bring your concerns about community to the Lord; ask for his work in your community and in the part you play in it, knowing that this matters to him: "Now you are the body of Christ, and each one of you is a part of it" (1 Corinthians 12:27).

A FINAL WORD

Onward

> *Therefore, since we are surrounded*
> *by such a great cloud of witnesses, let us throw off*
> *everything that hinders and the sin that so easily entangles.*
> *And let us run with perseverance the race marked out for us,*
> *fixing our eyes on Jesus, the pioneer and perfecter of faith.*

HEBREWS 12:1-2

WE ARE BROKEN PEOPLE LIVING IN A BROKEN WORLD. It can be easy to look at the problems we face and despair. After all, deep change, while possible, usually takes time and can be quite messy.

Faithful social action, however, isn't focused on change; it's focused first on faithfulness. God doesn't need more effective people, but he does want more obedient people. This reality is ultimately freeing because it means we're not expected to save the world, but we serve the God who is.

We all want to see change in the world, but as Christians we're called first and foremost to faithfulness. *And out of faithfulness comes fruitfulness.* So we trust that God remains at work. Even when his timing is mysterious, his ways are beyond our understanding and the outcomes don't always look like what we expected.

An Open Invitation

God *is* working and his Spirit *is* moving, of this I am assured.

We can see it through the enduring and ultimately successful campaign by William Wilberforce and the Clapham Sect to abolish slavery throughout the nineteenth-century British Empire.

We can see it through the powerful and courageous witness of Dietrich Bonhoeffer and the Confessing Church in the midst of brutal Nazi Germany.

We can see it through the spiritual revivals—such as the Great Awakenings in the United States—where millions of people came to follow Christ and great movements for social reform were birthed.

We can see it through the civil rights movement in the United States, which persevered in nonviolence and eventually triumphed over the unjust laws establishing racial inequality and segregation.

And we can see it in the remarkable ways God's people all across the world continue to make progress in spreading the gospel, promoting education, tackling the AIDS crisis, shining a light on human trafficking, advocating for the rights of women and minorities, building political momentum for immigration reform, helping communities adapt to climate change and so much more.

"The light shines in the darkness, and the darkness has not overcome it" (John 1:5). And it never will. Through Christ, change *is* possible, lives *can* be saved, society *can* be made more just and creation *can* be well cared for. The one who makes all things new desires us to be part of accomplishing his will here on earth as it is in heaven.

But it's up to us how we respond to God's calling and whether we accept his remarkable invitation to be part of building his kingdom. As Jesus taught, it's like a farmer going out to sow his seed:

As he was scattering the seed, some fell along the path, and the birds came and ate it up. Some fell on rocky places, where it did not have much soil. It sprang up quickly, because the soil was shallow. But when the sun came up, the plants were scorched, and they withered because they had no root. Other seed fell among thorns, which grew up and choked the plants. Still other seed fell on good soil, where it produced a crop—a hundred, sixty or thirty times what was sown. Whoever has ears, let them hear. (Matthew 13:4-9)

Unlike the seed that fell on the path and was devoured by the birds, may we understand the message about the kingdom and take it into our hearts.

Unlike the seed that fell in rocky places and became scorched by the sun, may the gospel of Christ grow deeply rooted in us so that we can persevere through whatever comes.

Unlike the seed that fell among thorns and was choked by the weeds, may we not be overcome by worldly anxieties and temptations, so that the Word can mature in us and bear fruit.

But like the seed sown on good soil, may God's reign and kingdom come alive in and through us, faithfully yielding a rich harvest for years to come.

HOPE IN CHRIST

A blessed day is coming when there will be no more need for social action. When we will no longer have to fight against injustice, because it will no longer exist. When there will be no more war, no more violence, no more racism, no more abuse, no more corruption, no more pollution, no more disease, no more pain, no more tears, no more brokenness, no more sin, no more evil and no more death.

There will be peace, and it will last. Shalom will finally be restored as all creation is healed, all relationships are restored and all things are reconciled to God (Colossians 1:20). Just as surely as Christ has risen

from the dead, so too will this day come to pass. It will be glorious, and
it will never end:

> No longer will there be any curse. The throne of God and of the
> Lamb will be in the city, and his servants will serve him. They
> will see his face, and his name will be on their foreheads. There
> will be no more night. They will not need the light of a lamp or
> the light of the sun, for the Lord God will give them light. And
> they will reign for ever and ever. (Revelation 22:3-5)

But that day is not here yet. So, as we wait longingly, we continue to
strive faithfully. We trust that, in the words of nineteenth-century missionary Hudson Taylor, "God's work done in God's way will never lack
God's supplies."[1] And that

> those who hope in the LORD
>   will renew their strength.
> They will soar on wings like eagles;
>   they will run and not grow weary,
>   they will walk and not be faint. (Isaiah 40:30-31)

ONWARD

Over the last ten years God has patiently led me on an uncomfortable but unforgettable journey of faith in action. It has been
filled with providential opportunities to witness him at work on
some of the world's darkest problems and to join in. I've tried in
these pages to share some of the stories and lessons from these
experiences, as well as wisdom and testimonies from those I've
come to know along the way.

Who knows what the next ten years or more will hold, either for
you or for me. But once we've chosen to follow Jesus, we put our hands
to the plow and we don't turn back (Luke 9:62). God never gave up on
saving us; we should never give up on serving him. Our calling is to
persevere in faithfulness; his promise is to extend his kingdom on

earth as it is in heaven. And we share in the confident hope of the apostle Paul that he who has begun a good work in us "will carry it on to completion until the day of Christ Jesus" (Philippians 1:6).

I leave you with this excerpt from a blessing written by Sister Ruth Fox of Sacred Heart Monastery in Richardton, North Dakota:

> May God bless you with **discontent** with easy answers, half truths, superficial relationships, so that you will live from deep within your heart.
>
> May God bless you with **anger** at injustice, oppression, abuse, and exploitation of people, so that you will work for justice, equality, and peace.
>
> May God bless you with **tears** to shed for those who suffer from pain, rejection, starvation and war, so that you will reach out your hand to comfort them and to change their pain to joy.
>
> May God bless you with the **foolishness** to think you can make a difference in this world, so that you will do the things which others tell you cannot be done.[2]

Amen. And may God find us faithful as we continue to press onward in Christ together.

FOR REFLECTION AND APPLICATION

1. Jesus taught us to pray "your will be done on earth as it is in heaven." So, pray that God will "bless you with discontent at easy answers, half-truths, superficial relationships, so that you will live from deep within your heart."

2. Pray that God will "bless you with anger at injustice, oppression, abuse, and exploitation of people, so that you will work for justice, freedom, and peace."

3. Pray that God will "bless you with tears to shed for those who suffer from pain, rejection, starvation and war, so that you will reach out your hand to comfort them and to change their pain to joy."

4. Pray that God will "bless you with the foolishness to think that you can make a difference in this world, so that you will do the things which others tell you cannot be done."

5. Pray, and at the same time hear this call to stand and take action with all possible vigor: "Therefore, since we are surrounded by such a great cloud of witnesses, let us throw off everything that hinders and the sin that so easily entangles. And let us run with perseverance the race marked out for us, fixing our eyes on Jesus, the pioneer and perfecter of faith" (Hebrews 12:1-2).

ACKNOWLEDGMENTS

MY PRAYER IS TO BE FAITHFUL WITH THE LIFE GOD HAS GIVEN ME. But there have been many times—even when writing this book—that I've struggled to persevere. Yet God remains faithful, and he has always surrounded me with loving family and friends. Without them my life and this book would be *a lot* worse off. May God bless you all for being such a blessing to me.

Special thanks to

Dad, Mom, Gram and Nat—for being family, supporting me in every endeavor and helping me find space to write this book.

Josh Martin—for your general longsuffering and the hours of research and writing help. Thank you for being a true brother.

Uncle Eric—for reviewing every stage and writing the discussion questions at the end of each chapter.

Uncle Ajith—for writing the foreword and for the friendship our families have shared over the years.

Fred and Linda Van Dyke—for your friendship and hospitality, which has only grown with time. Thank you for opening up your beautiful home for weeks on end so that I could retreat to a lake in the woods and write (while fishing on the side).

Ryan Cherry—for being a faithful friend, campaign manager and prayer partner.

My colleagues at the Evangelical Environmental Network—Mitch Hescox, Jim Ball and Alexei Laushkin—for all your support and friendship. Thanks in particular to Mitch for generously giving me time to write this book, and to Jim (and Kara) for your daily prayers throughout the process.

LaVonne and David Neff—for your friendship, support and hospitality. Thanks in particular to LaVonne for all the help and encouragement during the proposal stages of this book.

Amy Tracy—for your friendship, encouragement and insightful advice and edits. And for letting me include part of your remarkable story.

Matt Soerens, Mae Cannon, Jonathan Merritt, Tom Baker, Margot Starbuck and Tyler Wigg-Stevenson—for your friendship, connections and brainstorming help throughout this book project. David Vosburg, Ellen Morris and Becky Chen—for your valuable input during the cover design process.

The good folks at InterVarsity Press—for taking another chance with me. Thanks in particular to Jeff Crosby and Al Hsu for championing and guiding me through this process. Again. I'm very grateful for you.

Little Books of the Diocese of Saginaw for giving me permission to use "Prophets of a Future Not Our Own" as an epigraph, and Sr. Ruth Fox along with *Living Faith* for giving me permission to use her "Fourfold Benedictine Blessing" (also known as A Non-traditional Blessing) in the epilogue.

Peter Harris, Diane Swierenga, Rob Gallagher and Bruce Norquist—for being mentors, spiritual advisers and cheerleaders.

The Parkside Intentional Community, past and present—for your prayers and for persevering through this process with me.

Vince Morris, Ed Brown, Tom Rowley, Jonathan Kindberg, Jenn Carver, Cheryl Wenzlaff, the Norquists, the Norregaards, the Hickernells, and Janvier/Marie Jose/Christian and family—for your friendship, prayers and support through this process.

All who staffed and supported my campaign for US Congress—especially Lindy Scott and family, Bek Soen, Jesse Flannagan,

Bethany Erickson, Justin Fung, Don Kirchenberg, David Wilcox, Jeff Gimm, Angela Hager, Tom Castillo, Zach Stallard, Matthew Ely, Scott Plecki, Galen MaCrane, Bob and Maureen Doyle, Elise Bryson, Mike Murray, Marge Frens, Frank Goetz, Mark Witte, Bill and Dodie Lowe, and the Township organizations and PCs—you blessed and taught me so much. Aim High Vote Lowe!

The team at Young Evangelicals for Climate Action—you continue to inspire me.

The staff and trustees of the Au Sable Institute—I thank God whenever I think of you.

The Wheaton Chinese Alliance Church (and youth group)—for being my church family for over a decade.

Finally, to all who have shared their lives with me and allowed me to share your wisdom and stories in this book—thank you!

NOTES

Foreword by Ajith Fernando

[1]I still remain very active as a lay leader and local preacher in the church of my youth, the Methodist Church of Sri Lanka. The commitment to social action and justice in our denomination remains strong, but I rejoice in the revival of commitment to evangelism and in the growth of the church through the starting of faith communities among people previously unreached by the gospel message.

Begin Here

[1]Kenneth Untener, "Prophets of a Future Not Our Own," 1979. Rev. Untener was Bishop of the Diocese of Saginaw.

Chapter 1: Wait, Don't Give Up!

[1]Bethany Hoang, *Deepening the Soul for Justice* (Downers Grove, IL: InterVarsity Press, 2012), p. 27.

[2]John R. W. Stott, "John Stott: Four Ways Christians Can Influence the World," *Christianity Today,* October 20, 2011, p. 38.

[3]C. S. Lewis, "First and Second Things," in *God in the Dock: Essays on Theology and Ethics* (Grand Rapids: Eerdmans, 1994), p. 280.

[4]In particular, see Tyler Wigg-Stevenson, *The World Is Not Ours to Save* (Downers Grove, IL: InterVarsity Press, 2013).

[5]In particular, see Sandra Joireman, *Church, State, and Citizen: Christian Approaches to Political Engagement* (New York: Oxford University Press, 2009).

[6]Dietrich Bonhoeffer, quoted on the back cover of Eric Metaxas, *Bonhoeffer: Pastor, Martyr, Prophet, Spy* (Nashville: Thomas Nelson, 2011).

Chapter 2: Is Social Action Necessary?

[1]Tyler Wigg-Stevenson, *The World Is Not Ours to Save* (Downers Grove, IL: InterVarsity Press, 2013), p. 53.

[2]Raul Delgado, "Wheaton Persuades Students to Switch to Trayless Using

Fun Campaign," Bon Appétit, October 29, 2013, www.bamco.com/blog /wheaton-persuades-students-to-switch-to-trayless-using-fun-campaign.

[3]Dom Hélder Câmara, quoted in Zildo Rocha, *Helder, O Dom: uma vida que marcou os rumos da lgreja no Brasil* [Helder, the Gift: A Life That Marked the Course of the Church in Brazil], (Petrópolis, Brazil: Editora Vozes, 2000), p. 53. This is a translation of "Quando dou comida aos pobres chamam-me de santo. Quando pergunto por que eles são pobres chamam-me de comunista."

[4]Matthew Soerens and Jenny Hwang Yang, *Welcoming the Stranger* (Downers Grove, IL: InterVarsity Press, 2009).

[5]Jim Elliot, quoted in Elisabeth Elliot, *Shadow of the Almighty: The Life and Testimony of Jim Elliot* (New York: HarperCollins, 2009), p. 108. This statement by Jim Elliot was originally in his October 28, 1940, journal entry.

[6]Merrell Tuck, "Poverty Overview," World Bank, April 2013, http://go .worldbank.org/en/topic/poverty/overview.

Chapter 3: Overcoming Obstacles to Social Action

[1]Tim Keller, *Generous Justice* (New York: Penguin, 2010), p. 129.

[2]Tyler Wigg-Stevenson, *The World Is Not Ours to Save* (Downers Grove, IL: InterVarsity Press, 2013), p. 47.

[3]Ibid., p. 125.

[4]Frederick Buechner, *Wishful Thinking: A Theological ABC* (New York: Harper Row, 1973), p. 95.

[5]Alexia Salvatierra and Peter Heltzel, *Faith-Rooted Organizing* (Downers Grove, IL: InterVarsity Press, 2013), p. 87-88.

[6]Duane Litfin, personal communication, Feb 26, 2013; he's also said this in various chapel messages throughout the years.

[7]Steve Corbett and Brian Fikkert, *When Helping Hurts: How to Alleviate Poverty Without Hurting the Poor . . . and Yourself* (Chicago: Moody Publishers, 2012); and Robert D. Lupton, *Toxic Charity: How the Church Hurts Those They Help and How to Reverse It* (New York: HarperOne, 2011).

[8]See Matthew Soerens, *Welcoming the Stranger* (Downers Grove, IL: Inter-Varsity Press, 2009), or M. Daniel Carroll R., *Christians at the Border* (Grand Rapids: Baker Academic, 2008).

[9]Martin Luther King Jr., *Strength to Love* (Minneapolis: Fortress, 2010), p. 26.

[10]Margaret Philbrick, "When Your Calling Is Boring," *Relevant*, June 25, 2013,

www.relevantmagazine.com/life/when-your-calling-boring#XBOtDoxr
8bIZhXbX.99.

CHAPTER 4: RECONCILING EVANGELISM AND SOCIAL ACTION

[1]"Mortality and Global Health Estimates," World Health Organization, accessed February 18, 2014, www.who.int/gho/mortality_burden_disease/en.

[2]"Child Survival Fact Sheet: Water and Sanitation," UNICEF, June 4, 2004, www.unicef.org/media/media_21423.html. Statistics from 2012 report that approximately 2,000 children die per day from diarrhea-related diseases, and 88 percent of those "are due to poor drinking water, lack of sanitation and poor hygiene" (www.childinfo.org/water.html).

[3]"Injustice Today," International Justice Mission, accessed February 18, 2014, www.ijm.org/our-work/injustice-today.

[4]"Fast Facts: The Faces of Poverty," UN Millennium Project, 2006, www.un millenniumproject.org/documents/3-MP-PovertyFacts-E.pdf.

[5]"Global Christianity: A Report on the Size and Distribution of the World's Christian Population," PewResearch, December 19, 2011, www.pewforum .org/2011/12/19/global-christianity-exec.aspx.

[6]"Great Commission Statistics," Joshua Project, joshuaproject.net/great -commission-statistics.php.

[7]Thanks to the Rev. Dr. Jim Ball for helping me to articulate the contrasts between these two movements.

[8]"About the Lausanne Movement," Lausanne Movement, accessed February 18, 2014, www.lausanne.org/en/about.html.

[9]John Stott, *Balanced Christianity*, exp. ed. (Downers Grove, IL: InterVarsity Press, 2014), p. 51.

[10]Rowan Williams, "Archbishop Remembers John Stott," Dr. Rowan Williams (blog), July 28, 2011, http://rowanwilliams.archbishopofcanterbury.org /articles.php/2144/archbishop-remembers-john-stott.

[11]Andy Crouch, "Underrepresented at Cape Town," *Christianity Today*, October 22, 2010, http://blog.christianitytoday.com/ctliveblog/archives/2010/10 /im_in_cape_town.html.

[12]Chris Wright, ed., *The Cape Town Commitment* (Peabody, MA: Hendrickson, 2011), pt. 1, sec. 7a.

[13]Personal email, December 12, 2013.

[14]For the full comments and more on "The Price of Life" campaign at Ohio State University, see InterVarsity's "Ohio State University Price of Life Invitational"

video at http://vimeo.com/11820743 or visit http://osupriceoflife.org.

[15]Timothy Keller, *Generous Justice* (New York: Penguin, 2010), p. 189.

Chapter 5: Transcending the Culture Wars

[1]A fundamental difference between conservatives and progressives is that conservatives idealize the past and view the future as a threat to be guarded against, whereas progressives idealize the future and see the past in a negative light. Additionally, in his classic book *Culture Wars* (New York: Basic Books, 1992) renowned sociologist James Davison Hunter describes a key clash in ideology around the two ideals of freedom and justice. Conservatives emphasize freedom in economic terms and justice in personal morality, whereas progressives emphasize freedom in personal morality and justice in economic terms.

[2]Famous leaders in the religious right include Jerry Falwell, James Dobson, Ralph Reed, Pat Robertson and many others. Wikipedia has a detailed description of the "Christian Right" in the United States. See "Christian Right," http://en.wikipedia.org/wiki/Christian_right.

[3]"Election 2012 Post Mortem: White Evangelicals and Support for Romney," Pew Research, December 7, 2012, www.pewforum.org/2012/12/07/election -2012-post-mortem-white-evangelicals-and-support-for-romney.

[4]Os Guinness, *The Case for Civility: And Why Our Future Depends on It* (New York: Harper One, 2008), p. 84.

[5]Eric Hoffer, *The True Believer: Thoughts on the Nature of Mass Movements* (New York: Harper Perennial, 2002), p. 91.

[6]These resources include the Pew Annual Religion and Public Life Surveys, the Faith Matters Surveys, which are analyzed in Robert Putnam, *American Grace* (New York: Simon & Schuster, 2010), James Davidson Hunter, *To Change the World* (New York: Oxford University Press 2010), and David Kinnaman and Gabe Lyons, *unChristian* (Grand Rapids: Baker, 2007).

[7]For more on this research see Kinnaman and Lyons, *unChristian*. They've each followed this up: see Gabe Lyons, *The Next Christians* (New York: Doubleday Religion, 2010); and David Kinnaman, *You've Lost Me* (Grand Rapids: Baker, 2011).

[8]Ed Stetzer, "Prop 8, DOMA, and the Christian Response," *Christianity Today*, June 26, 2013, www.christianitytoday.com/edstetzer/2013/june /prop-8-doma-and-christian-response.html.

[9]Martin Luther King Jr., "Letter from Birmingham City Jail," in *A Testament of Hope: The Essential Writings and Speeches of Martin Luther King, Jr.*, ed.

James M. Washington (New York: HarperOne, 1986), pp. 289-302.

[10]Alexia Salvatierra and Peter Heltzel, *Faith-Rooted Organizing* (Downers Grove, IL: InterVarsity Press, 2014).

[11]One good resource is Richard Hughes, *Christian America and the Kingdom of God* (Champaign: University of Illinois Press, 2012) .

[12]Timothy Keller, *Generous Justice* (New York: Penguin, 2010), p. 21.

[13]K. Allan Blume, "'Guilty as Charged,' Cathy Says of Chick-fil-A's Stand on Biblical and Family Values," *Baptist Press*, July 16, 2012, www.bpnews.net /BPnews.asp?ID=38271; and Jena McGregor "Chick-fil-A President Dan Cathy Bites into Gay-Marriage Debate," *Washington Post*, July 19, 2012, www .washingtonpost.com/blogs/post-leadership/post/chick-fil-a-president-dan -cathy-bites-into-gay-marriage-debate/2012/07/19/gJQACrvzvW_blog.html.

[14]Shane L. Windmeyer, "Dan and Me: My Coming Out as a Friend of Dan Cathy and Chick-fil-A," *Huffington Post*, January 28, 2013, www.huffingtonpost.com /shane-l-windmeyer/dan-cathy-chick-fil-a_b_2564379.html.

[15]Ibid.

[16]Frederica Mathewes-Green, "Chasing Amy," *Christianity Today*, January 10, 2000, www.christianitytoday.com/ct/2000/january10/5.56.html; and Amy Tracy, "The Grace Escape," *Christianity Today*, March 7, 2008, www.chris tianitytoday.com/ct/2008/march/35.52.html.

[17]Personal email, November 29, 2012.

CHAPTER 6: RESTORING A FAITHFUL AGENDA

[1]See www.pbs.org/now/science/mercuryinfish.html.

[2]Records and summaries of campaign contributions are freely available on all members of Congress at www.opensecrets.org.

[3]Ben Geman, "Evangelical Group Holds Firm on 'Pro-life' Link to EPA Rule," *The Hill*, February 10, 2012, http://thehill.com/policy/energy-environment/209831 -evangelical-group-holds-firm-on-pro-life-link-to-epa-rule.

[4]Mitch Hescox, personal email, March 20, 2014.

[5]Wendell Berry, *Citizenship Papers* (Berkeley, CA: Counterpoint, 2004), p. 30.

[6]Ibid.

[7]Tyler Wigg-Stevenson, *The World Is Not Ours to Save* (Downers Grove, IL: InterVarsity Press, 2013), p. 172.

[8]*For the Health of the Nation* is an official NAE policy document and can be downloaded free from their website: www.nae.net/government-relations /for-the-health-of-the-nation.

Chapter 7: Love

[1]Adapted from 1 Corinthians 13:1-3, *The Message*.

[2]Martin Luther King Jr., *Where Do We Go from Here: Chaos or Community?* (Boston: Beacon, 1967), p. 62.

[3]Brother Lawrence, *The Practice of the Presence of God* (Benton, AR: Benton, 2012), p. 12.

[4]Ajith Fernando, *Reclaiming Love* (Grand Rapids: Zondervan, 2012), p. 48.

[5]Martin Luther King Jr., *Strength to Love* (Minneapolis: Fortress, 2010), p. 27.

[6]Tyler Wigg-Stevenson, *The World Is Not Ours to Save* (Downers Grove, IL: InterVarsity Press, 2013), p. 110.

[7]Andy Marin, quoted in Heather Sells, "Christian Outreach to Gays: I'm Sorry," *CBN News*, September 19, 2010, www.cbn.com/cbnnews/us/2010/august/missionarys-message-to-gays-im-sorry-/.

[8]David Kinnaman and Gabe Lyons, *unChristian* (Grand Rapids: Baker, 2008).

Chapter 8: Prophecy

[1]Darius Salter, *What Really Matters in Ministry: Profiling Pastoral Success in Flourishing Churches* (Grand Rapids: Baker, 1990), pp. 45, 50.

[2]Walter Brueggemann, *The Prophetic Imagination*, 2nd ed. (Minneapolis: Augsburg Fortress, 2001), pp. 116-17.

[3]Portions of this story are adapted from Ben Lowe, "Marching to Town Hall with Refugees and Immigrants," *Christianity Today*, July 9, 2013, www.christianitytoday.com/thisisourcity/7thcity/marching-to-town-hall-with-refugees-and-immigrants.html.

[4]"Glen Ellyn (village), Illinois," United States Census Bureau, accessed February 21, 2014, http://quickfacts.census.gov/qfd/states/17/1729756.html.

[5]Kristen Erikson, "Protecting Low Income Residents During Tax Increment Financing Redevelopment," *Washington University Journal of Law and Policy* 36 (2011), http://law.wustl.edu/journal/36/Erickson.pdf.

Chapter 9: Opposition

[1]Sometime after the election she did send an email apology.

[2]Abraham Lincoln, quoted in F. B. Carpenter, *Six Months at the White House with President Lincoln* (Bedford, MA: Applewood Books, 1866), p. 282.

[3]For more information on the Hope for the Holy Land initiative, visit www.worldvision.org/hope-for-the-holy-land.

[4]Personal conversation, July 13, 2013.

CHAPTER 10: IDOLATRY

[1]See Kyle Idleman, *Gods at War* (Grand Rapids: Zondervan, 2013), p. 117.
[2]Ibid., p. 22.
[3]Ibid., p. 24.
[4]Tyler Wigg-Stevenson, *The World Is Not Ours to Save* (Downers Grove, IL: InterVarsity Press, 2013), p. 60.
[5]A. W. Tozer, *The Pursuit of God* (Rockville, MD: Wildside, 2013), p. 39.
[6]Kent Carlson and Mike Lueken , *Renovation of the Church* (Downers Grove, IL: InterVarsity Press, 2011), p. 75.

CHAPTER 11: REPENTANCE

[1]Soong-Chan Rah, "A Time to Mourn," *Sojourners*, July 19, 2013, http://sojo .net/blogs/2013/07/19/time-mourn.

CHAPTER 12: SABBATH

[1]Portions of this section have been adapted from my review of *24/6: A Prescription for a Healthier, Happier Life*, by Matthew Sleeth, in *PRISM* 20, no. 3 (May-June 2013): 44.
[2]Bethany H. Hoang, *Deepening the Soul for Justice* (Downers Grove, IL: InterVarsity Press, 2012), p. 11.
[3]Matthew Sleeth, *24/6* (Carol Stream, IL: Tyndale, 2012), p. 52.

CHAPTER 13: CONTEMPLATION

[1]Bethany H. Hoang, *Deepening the Soul for Justice* (Downers Grove, IL: InterVarsity Press, 2012), p. 7.
[2]Ibid.. p. 11.
[3]Richard Lovelace, *Dynamics of Spiritual Life*, (Downers Grove, IL: InterVarsity Press 1979), p. 392.
[4]Hoang, *Deepening the Soul for Justice*, p. 33.
[5]Ronald J. Sider, *Doing Evangelism Jesus' Way* (Nappanee, IN: Evangel, 2003), pp. 37-38.
[6]Brother Lawrence, *The Practice of the Presence of God: The Best Rule of a Holy Life* (Radford, VA: Wilder, 2008), p. 24.

CHAPTER 14: COMMUNITY

[1]Eugene Peterson, *A Long Obedience in the Same Direction*, 20th anniv. ed. (Downers Grove, IL: InterVarsity Press, 2000), p. 175.
[2]I adapted this analogy from one that Henri Nouwen used to describe the

Christian life: "Sometimes I think of life as a big wagon wheel with many spokes. In the middle is the hub. Often in ministry, it looks like we are running around the rim trying to reach everybody. But God says, 'Start in the hub; live in the hub. Then you will be connected with all the spokes, and you won't have to run so fast'" (Henri Nouwen, "Moving from Solitude to Community," *Leadership*, spring 1995, www.christianitytoday.com/le/1995 /spring/5l280.html).

[3]Claiborne and Wilson-Hartgrove, *Becoming the Answer to Our Prayers* (Downers Grove, IL: InterVarsity Press, 2009), p. 51.

A FINAL WORD: ONWARD

[1]Hudson Taylor, quoted in Leslie T. Lyall, *A Passion for the Impossible: The Continuing Story of the Mission Hudson Taylor Began* (London: OMF Books, 1965), p. 37.

[2]Ruth Fox, "A Non-Traditional Blessing." Originally published as "A Mixed Blessing" in *Living Faith*, 1989. Used with permission.